MEMOIRS

OF THE

SCIENCE DEPARTMENT

TÔKIÔ DAIGAKU

(University of Tokyo)

No. 6

THE CHEMISTRY

OF

SAKE BREWING

BY

R.W. ATKINSON, B.Sc. (Lond.)
Professor of Analytical and Applied Chemistry in Tokio Daigaku

PUBLISHED BY TÔKIÔ DAIGAKU
TÔKIÔ

2541
(1881)

Published by

VintReads - 2018

www.vintreads.com

post@vintreads.com

ISBN 978-82-93684-21-3

TABLE OF CONTENTS

PREFACE

Previous to the year 1878 no scientific account of the brewing of sake had appeared, the principal papers which had been published being a translation by Professor J.J. Hofmann, of Leyden, of an article from the Japanese Encylopaedia, 1714, and a paper in the transactions of the German Asiatic Society of Japan by Dr. Hofmann, then Professor in the Medical School of the University of Tokyo. In December, 1878, Mr. O. Korschelt published an elaborate paper on the subject in the same transactions, in which he gave a detailed description of two processes used in Tokyo, and the results of special experiments made by himself, after which it seemed that very little more could be said. But continued study of the brewing-process has yielded results which enable us to explain with greater accuracy the chemical changes involved in the manufacture, and although much yet remains to be achieved, the present essay will, I trust, be accepted as another rung in the endless ladder of scientific investigation.

In carrying out this research I have been assisted in very various ways by a number of friends, all of whom it would be impossible to mention individually, but I should with reason incur the charge of ingratitude did I not put in the front rank Mr. Kato, President, and Mr. Hattori, Vice-President, of the University, to whom indeed the very existence of this memoir is owing. My thanks are also due to Mr. Jihei Kamayama and to Mr. Tobei Isuka, of Yushima, Tokyo, Proprietors of the koji and sake works, respectively; to Mr. Mansuke Izumi, of Nishinomiya, and to Mr. Shinyemon Konishi, of Itami, to all of whom I owe much valuable information.

To M. Pasteur I am indebted for permission to make use of plates 17, 18, and 19, taken from his "Etudes sur le Vin". Without the cordial cooperation of my assistant, Mr. Nakazawa, my task would have been much more difficult, and thus publicly I desire to acknowledge my indebtedness to him. Plate 16 I owe to Professor Ewing, and Professor Cooper has with the greatest kindness looked over the proofs for me.

The substance of Part I of this memoir was communicated to the Royal Society of London in a Paper read on 10th March 1881.

The printing of the memoir was carried out at the Government Printing Office (Insetsu Kiyoku), and the plates were engraved by the Gengendo Engraving Company.

The accompanying French (metric) and English equivalents of the Japanese weights and measures used in the text will prove of assistance to those who are not familiar with them.

Table 1: Japanese, Metric, and English Weights

Japanese	Metric	English
1 kuwamme (kw.)	= 3.75 kilos	= 8.28 pounds.
1 shaku	=0.30303 meter	= 0.9942 ft.
1 cho (= 10 tan)	= 0.99174 hectare	= 2.45 acres
1 koku (= 10 to = 100 sho = 1000 go)	= 180.39 liters	= 4.963 bushels = 39.7 gallons
1 yen (paper) (= 100 sen)		about 2s-6d

R.W.A.

University of Tokyo,

Japan May 1881

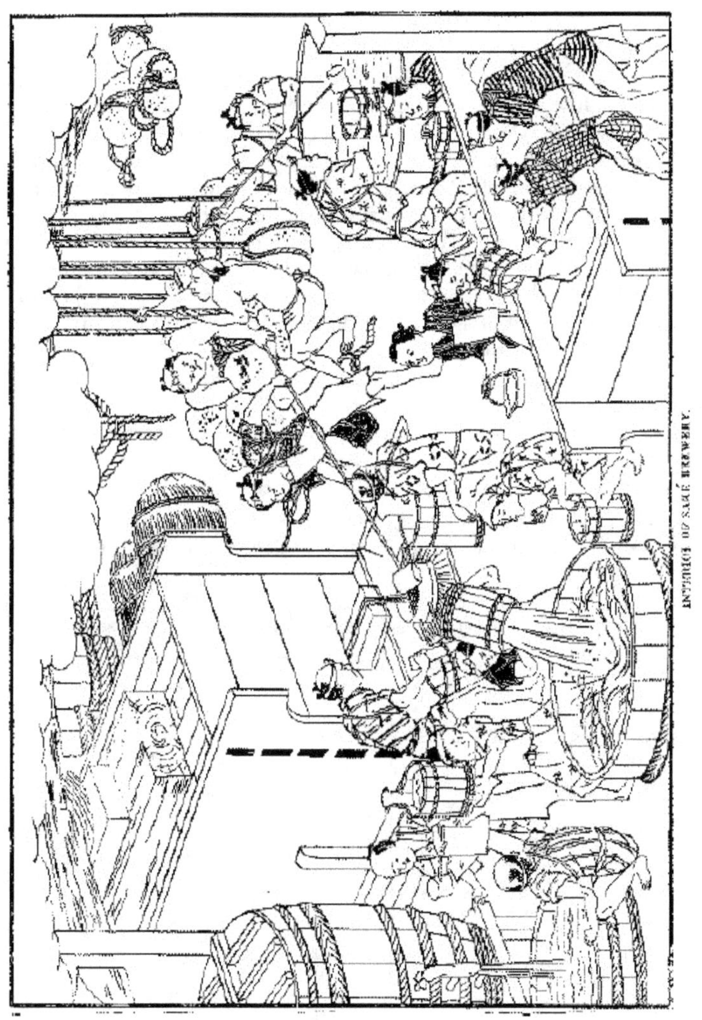

INTERIOR OF SAKÉ BREWERY.

INTRODUCTION

It is probably impossible now to ascertain when the art of brewing first became known to the Japanese. Tradition ascribes its introduction to some emigrants from Korea about the end of the third century, who doubtless obtained the knowledge from China where it had long been practices. How improvements were introduced we can only surmise, but it is known that about the end of the 15th century, the two districts of Itami and Ikeda had established their superiority over all others, a position which, together with Nishinomiya, they hold to this day. About 300 years ago a very important improvement was effected relating to the preservation of the sake which, in the hot months of summer very quickly became undrinkable. This consisted in heating the sake to such a temperature that the hand could not bear it, but, although answering the purpose for a time, it did not suffice in the manner in which the heating was carried out to permit the liquid to be kept for any lengthened period. Nor has any important alteration in the process of manufacture been introduced since that time notwithstanding the trouble entailed upon the brewer by the repeated heating of the sake which is necessary, but it is hoped that the suggestions made in this memoir may have the effect of directing attention to the important and efficient process introduced by M. Pasteur for preserving wine.

I am indebted to Mr. Shigetoshi Yoshiwara, Vice-Minister of Finance, for the following statement of the quantity of the various kinds of alcoholic liquids produced in the year ending September 30th, 1880.

Table 2: Alcohol Production for Year Ending September 30, 1880

	Tax per koku	No. of koku	Revenue in yen
Ordinary sake (seishu)	1 yen	5,015,084	5,015,084
Turbid sake (nigorizake)	0.3 yen	65,494	19,648
White sake (shiro-zake)	2 yen	1,500	3,000
Sweet sake for cooking (mirin)	2 yen	38,569	77,138
Liquer (meishu)	3 yen	3,615	10,845
Spirit (shochu)	1.5 yen	83,708	125,562
		5,207,970	5,251,277
Fees from sale of licences to brewers and retail dealers			1,208,293
Total revenue derived from alcoholic liquors			6,459,570 yen

The estimated amount of revenue from alcoholic liquers for the year ending September 30th, 1881 is 10,795,025 yen, the total estimated revenue being 56,616,907 yen. The former estimate is much greater than the actual yield of the past year, owing to the considerable changes which have been made both in the amounts and in the mode of collecting the taxes.* The amount of the different kinds of sake given in the table above is 5,207,970 koku, or 206,756,409 gallons, but this number does not express the total quantity consumed, for without any doubt, much sake which is not taxes, is prepared in private houses in the country. Taking into consideration only the amount of ordinary sake used, say 5 million koku, or 198 million gallons, the consumption corresponds to 6 gallons per head per annum reckoning the population at 33 millions. If it were diluted twice so as to be about the same strength as beer, the consumption would be doubled, that is 12 gallons a head, whilst the consumption of beer in England averages 34 gallons per head, nearly three times as much as in Japan. The brewing of sake is, therefore, relatively of less importance than that of beer in England, and this is doubtless to be ascribed to the enormous consumption of tea, which serves at all times, in summer and in winter, as the national beverage.

The study of the chemical reactions involved in the brewing process described in the following pages has brought to light a fact of some importance relating to the physiology of plants, vis. that the growth of a mold over the surface of perfectly dead rice grains causes a change in the character of the albumenoid matter of the grain resembling that which results from the germination of the embryo of similar grains. I cannot omit here to draw attention to the mutual advantage to be derived from an association of workers in industrial and in pure science; the cooperation cannot but be of the greatest utility on the one hand, by suggesting new subjects for research to the theoretical worker, and on the other, in aiding the practical man to attain the best results possible. The student of science in Japan has a wide field before him; that system of isolation which has prevented the introduction of Western knowledge till within the last quarter of a century has not been entirely fruitless, for it has resulted in the development of industrial processes which are as novel and interesting to the European as those of the latter are to Japanese. The scientific students of the university and colleges of Japan need not, therefore, look very far in order to find subjects that require investigation and explanation, and this search will, without doubt, add largely to the sum total of existing knowledge.

---

*. The estimated revenue derived from the production and sale of alcoholic liquors given above differs greatly from that which appears in the Estimates of the Minister of Finance for the year ending June 30th 1881. The number there given is 5,965,029 yen, or very little more than one-half the estimates for the year ending three months later. The explanation of the difference lies in the fact that since the Estimates of the Minister of Finance were published the taxes have been doubled.

PART I: KOJI

Chapter 1. Rice

The grain from which alcohol is produced in Japan is the same as that which forms the staple article of diet for all classes, vis. rice, and its cultivation employs the labor of the greater number of the population. According to the Official Catalogs of the Japanese Exhibits at Philadelphia in 1876, and at Paris in 1878, the total area of paddy land is 1,611,130 cho (3,947,268 acres), and the yield of rice amounts to 28,000,000 koku (138,964,000 bushels), giving an average yield of a little more than 35 bushels per acre. The numbers given by General LeGendre in his work "Progressive Japan," are larger than these, but are said to have been obtained from the Finance department, being the results of more recent surveys. He says "According to recent surveys (1874-78) the area of rice fields in Japan is 2,539,090 cho and 47 tan, and the area of other fields (Miscellaneous cultures) is 1,732,449 cho and 73 tan (Figures procured at the Okura-Sho)."[*] Further on he gives the total quantity of rice produced as 34,394,787 koku, a number also furnished by the Okura-Sho (Finance Department), and from these the average yield of rice is calculated to be a little more than 27 bushels per acre. These numbers include rice of all kinds, several hundred varieties, but of these there are only three which are sufficiently well marked to particularize. One variety is called *Okabo*, and is grown in dry fields, whilst the two others, common rice (*uruchi*), and glutinous rice (*mochigome*) are grown in paddy fields. It is said that the upland rice (*okabo*) is well suited for brewing purposes because it leaves very little residue, but I have had no experience of its use for that purpose, that which is almost universally employed being the common rice (*uruchi*). Glutinous rice is never used for the brewing of sake, the reason given being that the liquid prepared from it would rapidly putrefy, but another possible reason is its greater cost.

The best qualities of rice come from Mino, Higo, Ise, Owari, Totomi, and Hizen. The next best are from Boshiu, Tamba, Tajima, and the third quality from Kadzusa, Shimosa, Musashi, and Kaga.

The following analyses of the two kinds of rice were made in the University laboratory.

Table 3: Analyses of Hulled Rice of Various Years

		Common Rice							Glutinous Rice		
		Ise 1877	Mino 1877	Banshiu 1877	Ise 1879	Mino 1879	Sendai 1879	1880	Koshi-gaya 1877	Kazai 1877	1879
	Water	11.96	18.02	12.86	11.79	11.54	12.63	11.96	12.41	12.60	10.56
water soluble	Sugar and Dextrin	3.22	3.52	6.45	1.49	2.60	3.94	1.99	4.78	4.40	4.06
	Ash	.72	.87	1.12	1.17	1.22	.88	.58	1.45	1.05	1.12
	Albumenoids				1.04	.98		1.76			.74
insoluble in water	Albumenoids	4.79	5.07	5.13	5.74	4.99	5.69	5.42	4.30	4.30	5.62
	Starch	74.69	72.52	69.23	73.31	73.73	72.54	73.31	72.80	72.81	70.15
	Cellulose	2.98	3.13	3.27	2.56	2.54	2.35	3.68	2.79	2.67	3.63
	Fat	.90	1.21	1.85	1.27	1.57	.94	1.07	1.30	1.18	2.48
	Ash	.74	.66	.09	.14	.10	.54	.22	.16	.99	.38
		100.00	100.00	100.00	98.51	99.27	99.51	99.99	100.00	100.00	98.74

No essential difference in chemical composition between the two kinds of rice is disclosed by the foregoing analyses, but the two grains can be distinguished at the first glance after removing the husk, the common rice being translucent, whilst the glutinous rice is white and opaque. The name "glutinous rice" is given to the latter, doubtless, from the peculiarity it possesses of forming, when steamed and beaten, pasty lumps of great tenacity, a property which is not shared by the common rice. It is a similar property to that possessed by wheaten flour, and in that grain is due to the presence of a peculiar nitrogenous body galled "gliadin" which is not present to any marked extent in other grains. This substance is soluble in hot alcohol and if it were present in glutinous rice might be expected to be found in the alcoholic solution, but experiments made for that purpose have not shown any great difference between the two kinds of rice in the proportion of albumenoids dissolved by alcohol. Nor is there any difference in the amounts soluble in cold water; the only essential difference I have been able to detect is in the action of iodine solution upon the flour, that of common rice being colored deep blue, like starch, and that of the glutinous variety red, like dextrin. The cause of this difference more probably lies in the nature of the albumenoids than in the proportion of dextrin.

The weight of a given bulk of rice varies considerably according to the way in which it is packed, and in calculating the weights of rice used in sake-brewing from the volume, I have taken what may be considered a fair average, vis. 40 kuwamme per koku. This is founded upon the following direct weighings. One sho of the specified kinds of rice was loosely placed in the measure, and without shaking, carefully levelled; each number is the mean of seven weighings.

		Weight of one sho (grams)	Weight of one koku (kuwamme)
Common Rice	Kazai	1391	37.03
	Sendai	1346	35.83
	Mino	1379	36.72
	Ise	1401	37.30
Glutinous rice	Kazai	1394	37.12
	Mean		36.80

When the rice was tightly packed, that is, after being well shaken down, the average weight of one koku was 42 kuwamme, and as a rough average between the weights when loosely and when tightly packed, 40 kuwamme per koku will not be far from the truth.

The rice grain is a complex structure formed of a great many distinct parts, some of which can be readily parted by ordinary mechanical appliances, while others can only be separated by special means. Of the former is the hard outer coat, itself composed of several different parts, which is generally removed by the farmer as chaff before the rice is sent into the market. The hulled grain, in the form in which it is bought for food consists of three easily discernible parts, a thin, yellowish skin on the outside (the testa), within this the white starchy matter which constitutes the nutritious part of the grain (the endosperm), and at the lower end a portion of a different appearance, usually horny and shrivelled looking (the embryo). Immediately below the testa the cells of the endosperm do not differ in general appearance from those in the interior, but the greater part of the albumenoid matter of the endosperm is accumulated in these cells. An excellent test for the presence of albumenoids is mercuric nitrate; if a section of a grain of rice be steeped in such a solution those portions which contain albumenoid matter become colored rice, whilst the rest of the grain remains uncolored. When a thin slice of the unwhitened grain is thus treated the cells forming the testa have a somewhat greenish color and can be sharply distinguished from the layer immediately within, which is deeply colored red. This coloration extends inwards for a distance a little greater than the thickness of the test, but the form of the cells thus colored does not appear to be different from the remainder of those forming the endosperm, and which assume no coloration. In a similar section of whitened rice the outer layer of greenish, square cells is not seen, and the edges present a jagged appearance, but the outer cells are as strongly colored red as before, showing that only a small portion, if any, of the cells containing nitrogenous matter has been removed. In fact, the thickness of the layer colored red cannot be said to have perceptibly diminished. The red coloration is not uniform but is distributed over numerous points, being stronger near the testa and becoming fainter away from it; under a high power distinct points of red matter can be distinguished; these are the aleurone grains.

When the rice grain is whitened the testa is removed by beating, and analyses show that the bran so obtained contains much more nitrogen than the average of the entire hulled grain. The two following analyses are taken from a paper on "The Agricultural Chemistry of Japan" by Prof. Kinch.*

	A	B
Water	10.96	11.05
Ash	9.11	9.22
Oil	13.20	15.50
Fibre	7.66	8.60
Albumenoids	13.41	13.55
Soluble carbohydrates	45.66	42.08
	100.0	100.0

These analyses show that the ash, oil, fibre, and albumenoids are contained in large proportions in the bran. Together with the testa, which is mainly fibre, or cellulose, the embryo is removed, and it is from that source that most of the fat and nitrogenous matter is derived. Notwithstanding the large percentage of albumenoid matter contained in the bran, that in the whitened rice has not very greatly diminished: thus in one specimen which contained 7.4 percent before cleaning, afterwards 6.9 percent was found, the proportion of moisture being the same in each. As the bran contains so much nitrogenous matter it might have been expected that the grain after whitening would have shown a marked diminution; that it does not do so is owing to the fact that the whitened grains are selected, those which are unbroken being separated from those which have been much broken. Thus there result on the one hand grains broken into minute portions containing very little nitrogen, and sold to the same maker, on the other, the unbroken, whitened grains containing still almost all the protein matter of the endosperm, and deprived of testa and embryo which together form the bran (*nuka*), and contain the largest percentage of albumenoids.

The following analyses of the whitened rice grain are given because from them the samples of koji, the composition of which is given afterwards (see Table 8) were prepared.

A is the rice used for making koji at the Yushima works; B is the rice used at the Tokyo brewery in the operations described in Part II.

Table 4: Composition of Whitened Rice Dried at 100° C.

			A	B
Insoluble in water	Starch		82.27 %	82.14 %
	Cellulose		4.79	3.02
	Fat		.49	1.12
	Ash		.46	.16
	Albumenoids	7.5	} 9.45	8.82
Soluble in water	Albumenoids	1.95		
	Dextrose and Dextrine		1.91	3.97
	Ash		.63	.77
			100.00	100.00
	Water		12.70	12.19

---

*. Progressive Japan. Note at the foot of the table given at the end.

*. Trans. Asiat. Soc. Japan, VIII. 393.

Chapter 2. Preparation of Koji

Starch is a substance insoluble in water and incapable of undergoing fermentation directly, that is, of being converted into alcohol. In beer-making countries the conversion of the starch into a sugar from which alcohol can be produced is effected by the use of malt, a body formed by allowing the embryo of the barley grain to become partially developed, by which a change in the character of the grain occurs, as the result of which it becomes possessed of certain properties attributed to the existence of a hypothetical substance known as "diastase". The peculiarity of "diastase" is that it is a body containing nitrogen and having the power of rendering thick starch-paste liquid owing to the formation from it of the sugar maltose together with dextrin. Other kinds of diastase occur, as for example in the saliva, and in the pancreas, and these forms, although they resemble in some respects the diastase contained in malt differ from it in other particulars. Thus, the diastase of malt is not able to cause maltose to take up water and so be converted into dextrose, but both the diastase of the saliva and of the pancreas effect the hydration of maltose and change it into dextrose. It is evident, therefore, that different kinds of diastase exist, and that it is not one substance only which possesses these properties. As the material koji is employed in the manufacture of sake, and as it is used for the same purpose as malt in beer breweries it becomes necessary to examine it in some detail that we may ascertain how far it agrees with, and how far it differs from other similar bodies.

Koji is prepared both in breweries and in special works, as it is used for various purposes besides sake making. It will be most convenient for us to examine the mode of manufacture in the special koji works, as there will be found the conditions essential to its successful production more readily than in the sake breweries. I am especially indebted to Mr. Jihei Kamayama of Yushima, Tokyo, for much information as well as for permission to investigate at his works the whole process of manufacture.

The essential part of the process is carried out in long narrow passages cut in the solid clay about 15 or 20 feet below the surface of the ground. The object of this is to have a chamber which being once heated will not easily lose its heat either by radiation or by conduction. That this result is produced by cutting the chambers in the clay is shown by the constancy of temperature which they are found to possess even when considerable changes take place in the temperature of the outer air. Clay is a very bad conductor of heat, and it is practically impossible for heat to be communicated either to or from these passages through the clay. The passages are about 25 or 30 feet in length, and each set is reached through a very low and narrow one---made so for the purpose of preventing as much as possible an exchange between the outer and inner air. The opening passage is not more than between 3 and 4 feet high and about 4 feet wide, and is usually closed with mats. It is approached by descending a shaft from the ground above, and at the other end it opens into a passage of somewhat larger dimensions, from which two others branch off nearly at right angles. It is in these innermost parts that the highest temperature is maintained. In the sake-breweries the warm chambers are less carefully constructed, being built near the surface of the ground of wooden planks coated with mud and thickly covered over with straw mats. This is evidently a less perfect method of keeping in the heat than that adopted in the koji works proper. Having described the apparatus used we may now consider how the rice is treated. It is brought to the works husked but not cleaned, and the process of cleaning or whitening, is done by the manufacturers. This consists in removing that thin outer skin, the testa, which, as we have seen, contains a large proportion of cellulose and mineral matter. It is removed by the brewers, as they say, because it would render the liquid brewed very liable to putrefy. In removing the bran the rice suffers a considerable loss of weight, owing not only to the loss of the testa, but also to the fact that many of the grains become broken and are rejected on that account. In most places the cleaning is effected by human labor. The rice to be cleaned is placed in a wooden mortar sunk in the ground, and a heavy wooden hammer supported upon a fulcrum is so arranged that on pressing down the side of the lever away from the mortar and then removing the pressure, the heavy end of the lever falls by its own weight into the mortar. As it falls it causes the grains of rice to rub against one another and so the skin becomes scraped off. The loss of weight varies according to the degree to which the cleaning is carried; that which is used for the preparation of koji and of moto (called *moto-mi*) loses from 30 to 40 percent of its volume, whilst the *kake-mi*, used in the stages designated *soye*, *naka*, and *shimai*, is not so thoroughly cleaned and loses only about 25 percent of its volume. The numbers given are, of course, only approximate for, in every operation the percentage of loss must be different. The pounded mass is separated into three portions---the whole grains---the broken grains, and the bran. The whole grains are employed in the manufacture of koji and sake, the broken grains are sometimes made into an inferior kind of koji, but generally, like the bran, are sold to other persons. The amount of bran obtained is said to be about 3 kuwamme (25 pounds) for every koku (4.96 bushels) of rice cleaned.

In some works (sake-works) steam power is employed to work the cleaners, and in other places water power is used.

The rice is next placed in a tank, covered with water, and from time to time trodden upon by the workmen, the water being frequently changed. The fine dust which was adherent to the grain is carried away by the water, but the amount of matter thus lost, although sufficient to make the water milky is not known. After this washing the grains is left in steep for one night by which it becomes quite soft and is ready for steaming. The object of the steeping is merely to render the grain soft so that the subsequent steaming may be as short as possible. It is therefore, not analogous to the steeping of the barleygrain in making malt, an operation which is required to promote the germination of the embryo. In the case under consideration, indeed, the embryo has been completely destroyed by the rough beating, and no subsequent germination is possible. It is important to remember this, so that it may be clearly understood in what respects the manufacture of koji differs from that of malt. But even were the embryo not removed by the process of cleaning, it would be completely killed by the next operation, that of steaming. The soaked rice is placed in a large tub which is provided with a false bottom covered with cloth; the tub is then fixed upon an iron boiler full of water. When the water boils the steam passes through an opening in the true bottom of the tub, and as it ascends through the rice which is placed upon the cloth covering the fast bottom, it heats the grain and causes the starch to become gelatinized. The grains of steamed-rice are flexible and of a horny appearance, and must be the same throughout. In this state the rice is called *mi*. It is now spread out upon mats to cool, and during this time the workmen prevent the grains cohering by rubbing them between their hands. When the temperature has fallen to about 29°C the foreman mixes with the rice a small quantity of *tane*, a yellowish powder consisting of the spores of a fungus described by the late Mr. Ahlburg under the name of Eurotium oryzae (Ahlb).[*] The quantity employed is not exactly the same in different works, but averages about 3cc to 4 to (72 liters) of rice.

The subsequent operations vary a little in different works but not in any essential particulars. I shall, therefore, only describe them as carried out in the koji works at Yushima, Tokyo.

The spores are in the first place thoroughly mixed with two or three handfuls of the rice, and this mixture is then scattered over the whole quantity of steamed rice; the corners of the mats are turned up so as to collect the whole into a heap in the middle which is afterwards again spread out, and these operations are repeated several times to ensure that the spores shall be uniformly distributed. The rice mixed with fungus spores is then carried below to the front part of the chambers where the temperature is not high, and is there allowed to remain one day covered with mats. On the second day the temperature of the mass is about 25 or 26°C so that it is rather lower than when the spores were mixed with it. About noon of the second day (calling that on which the admixture with spores took place the first day) the rice is put into baskets and carried above where it is sprinkled with water. In the evening of that day the mixture is spread out in thin layers upon wooden trays called *koji-buta* which are carried to the innermost part of the subterranean passage and placed upon the floor underneath the benches which bear the koji of the third day. The trays are allowed to remain in this position from about 5 p.m. on the second day until about 5 a.m. on the third day, by which time the previous batch of koji on the benches has been removed, and the new batch is then put in its place. The mixture of rice and spores which was previously spread out in a think layer over the tray is at this time (5 a.m. third day) collected into a heap on each tray and left until between 9 and 10 a.m. During this time the temperature rises considerably and, by the vegetation of the fungus, the grains are bound together. In order to prevent the temperature rising so high as to injure the vitality of the plant, the workmen cools the mass by spreading it out in a thin layer and leaving it for some time. After it has become somewhat cooler he again collects it into heaps and leaves it until about 1 p.m. at which time it has once more attained a temperature nearly as high as at 9 or 10 a.m. after which it is spread out and repeatedly worked with the hands during the rest of the day. Between 8 o'clock in the evening of the third day and 5 a.m. of the fourth day the fungus still continues to grow, sufficiently to bind the whole mass together and to the tray. At 5 a.m. it is removed from the chamber and preserved on the trays until required for use.

In the manufacture of koji for sake-making the sprinkling with water on the second day is omitted, and the project is then called *ki-koji* (raw koji).

The formation of koji is an illustration of the growth of the mycelium of a fungus which uses the starch of the rice grain as food. In plants which possess chlorophyll and develop in sunlight two processes go on, assimilation and respiration. The former is accompanied by a fixation of carbon contained in carbonic acid under the influence of the sun's rays, and by the simultaneous liberation of oxygen. In this way the majority of plants add to their substance. At the same time the second process, respiration, goes on, but to a smaller extent than the former: it consists of an oxidation of the tissues of the plant, carbonic acid being liberated. This is the only process which goes on in plants destitute of chlorophyll, the green coloring matter of plants, and it can be well observed to take place in the growth of the koji fungus. This process of respiration, or oxidation, as a chemist might call it, is accompanied by a remarkable development of heat sufficient to keep the temperature of the koji and of the chamber very high. The following temperature observations will show this---the first series was made in spring when the amount of koji being made was very small, and the outside temperature not very much below that of the chamber. In the second series of observations, made in December, the differences are much greater, the temperature of the outside air being very low, and that of the koji much higher. During the month in which these observations were made the amount of material produced is very large, and the chambers are kept fully worked: it is owing to this circumstance that the differences of temperature between the koji and that of the chamber are so much more marked than in May.

Table 5: Temperatures of Koji and Chambers in May. Koji of the Third Day Only

Date	Hour	Temperature of the outer air	Temperature of the koji chamber		Temperature of the koji (3rd day)
			Minimum	Maximum	
May 18th	8 a.m.	55.3° F.	72° F.	76° F.	No koji
	6 p.m.	61.8	72	74	
May 19th	7 a.m.	59.0	72	77	89.6° F.
	8 p.m.	64.0	74	76	
May 20th	8 a.m.	57.7	76	77	84.2
	9 p.m.	64.6	75	77	
May 21st	7 a.m.	60.5	75	76	
	9 p.m.	65.0	74	76	86
May 22nd	9 a.m.	68.6	75	77	86
	9 p.m.	60.0	76	79	89.8
May 23rd	7 a.m.	65.5	77	88	
	8 p.m.	65.0	79	82	95
May 24th	7 a.m.	64.0	80	81	102
	8 p.m.	66.5	78	80	86

A careful examination of the second series of temperature observations will enable us to trace the growth of the fungus very clearly. The temperatures of the koji at various times in the day have been arranged and are given in the table below.

Until 1 p.m. in every case the temperature of the koji is above 100° F., and after 1 p.m. in every case it falls below that point. The period of most active growth is, therefore, in the morning, and corresponds with the time during which the material is heaped up in masses. The effect of opening out the masses of koji will be best seen in the temperatures taken on Dec. 6th. At 8 a.m. the temperature was 106.6° F. and it continued to rise a little until between 9 a.m. and 10 a.m. when the workman broke open the heaps and spread them out.

The temperature taken at 10 a.m. shows that the mass had cooled down 5.6° F. After this the mixture was again made up into heaps and at 1 p.m. the temperature had again rise, though not quite so high as at 8 a.m. After the heaps have been broken down between 1 p.m. and 2 p.m. the rice continues to cool; on the 5th the temperature at 2 p.m. was 91.9° and at 8 p.m. had fallen to 88.8°F. The object, therefore, of the working of the mass is not so much to prevent the grains becoming too much matted together as to regulate the activity of the growth of the plant. If the grains were allowed to remain heaped up during the whole time, there would be a danger of the temperature rising to too high a point, and perhaps rendering the product useless, whilst if the grains were never collected into heaps, the temperature would not rise sufficiently high to allow the growth to go on vigorously.

Table 6: Temperatures of Koji and Chambers in December. Koji of the Third Day Only

Date	Hour	Temperature of the outer air	Temperature of the koji chamber			Temperature of the koji (3rd day)
			Minimum	Maximum	Observed	
December 5th	8 a.m.	40.7° F.	-	-	82° F.	104.8° F.
	2 p.m.	49.5	82° F.	83° F.	82	91.9
	8 p.m.	42.5	81	83	81	88.8
December 6th	8 a.m.	41.5	80	83	83	106.6
	10 a.m.	44.7	81.6	82	81.6	101.0
	1 p.m.	50.0	81	82.5	81.5	104
December 7th	9 a.m.	38.5	80	82.5	81.5	104.2
	2 p.m.	51.0	80.5	82	81.5	93.6
December 8th	8 a.m.	37.5	79	82.5	80	100.0

Table 7: Temperature of Koji on Third Day

Hour	Dec. 5	Dec. 6	Dec. 7	Dec. 8
8 a.m.	104.8° F.	106.6 ° F.	-	100.0 ° F.
9 a.m.	-	-	104.2° F,	-
10 a.m.	-	101.0	-	-
1 p.m.	-	104.0	-	-
2 p.m.	91.9	-	93.6	-
8 p.m.	88.8	-	-	-

The amount of heat generated during the growth of the fungus is remarkable, and will be best appreciated from the observations made in December. At that time the temperature of the open air in the shade varied between 38° and 51° F., whilst in the subterranean chamber the temperature of the air was very nearly constant and very much higher than that of the open air. The growing chamber is not artificially heated except at starting—that is, after having been disused for a considerable time. It is then heated by the introduction of barrels containing hot water, but after that, all the heat it receives is derived from the combustion of the rice, and the liberation of its carbon and hydrogen in the form of carbonic acid and water. That carbonic acid is formed in large quantity is shown by the rapid removal of the oxygen from a confined portion of air by the actively growing plant. A handful of the mixture on the trays was put into a bottle holding about 3 liters of air, and the bottle was then tightly closed with a cork through which tubes passed by means of which a sample of the air in the bottle could be forced out and collected for analysis. During the time the bottle remained in the chamber the ends of these tubes were closed with aoutchouc tubes and pinch-cocks. The bottle was allowed to remain at the temperature of the chamber for four hours, at the end of which time it was found that the whole of the oxygen in the three liters of air had been replaced by carbonic acid. The grains of rice in the bottle remained loose, whilst those on the trays exposed to the free air of the chamber were matted together. From this it may be inferred that the quantity of oxygen contained in the bottle was insufficient to generate the heat required by the fungus for growth, which, therefore, ceased as soon as all the oxygen was consumed.

The oxidation which goes on during the growth of the fungus, and by which the heat is generated, is effected mainly at the expense of the starch contained in the cells of the grain. Figure 2 represents a section of a grain of koji cut perpendicularly to the long axis, and shows that the cellular divisions at the circumference are almost lost, whilst in the center they are pretty distinct. Very few grains of starch, however, can be distinguished, only those which have resisted gelatinization during the operation of steaming: the starch is there, but cannot be distinguished, on account of its homogeneity. The following analysis of koji (A and B) will indicate its general composition, although as will be explained later on, the amount of the soluble matter varies under different treatment even with the same specimen a fact which accounts for the large percentage of starch in one specimen and the small amount in the other. The composition is given of the material after deducting the percentage of moisture lost by drying at 100°C.

Table 8: Composition of Koji Dried at 100° C.

		A	B
Soluble in water (A) 37.76% (B) 69.45%	Dextrose	25.02 %	58.10 %
	Dextrin	3.88	4.41
	Soluble ash	0.52	0.54
	Soluble Albumenoids	8.34 9.84	6.40 8.23
Insoluble in water	Insoluble Albumenoids	1.50	1.83
	Insoluble ash	0.09	0.04
	Starch	56.00	26.2
	Cellulose	4.20	1.94
	Fat	0.43	0.50
		99.98	99.96
	Water in original koji	25.82	28.10

Comparing these with the analyses of whitened rice given on page 10 it will be observed that the amount of starch present is much reduced. This is due to its conversion into dextrose and dextrin, which has been mainly effected during the solution in water, owing to an active agent contained in the koji of which more will be said hereafter. The percentage of starch which would correspond to the dextrose, dextrin. and starch given in the first analysis is 82.4%, a number very closely agreeing with that which the rice dried at 100° C actually contained. The actual loss of material during the growth of the fungus cannot be determined, therefore, by an analysis of the koji, although the increase in the total amount of albumenoids indicates that there has been a loss of some of the other constituents of the grain. The large proportion of soluble albumenoids will strike every one, but as this is connected with the existence of a kind of "diastase" contained in the koji, it will be referred to in connection with the properties of that body.

The loss of material caused by the growth of the fungus is evident when we consider the weight of koji formed from a given weight of rice. Mr. Jihei Kamayama was kind enough to make careful weighings of the rice used and of the resulting koji. The result obtained was that 3 to of whitened rice which weighed 11.43 kuwamme yielded 12.38 kuwamme of koji, or 100 parts by weight of the rice gave 108.3 parts by weight of koji. The rice contained 14.2% of water, and the koji contained 29.5%, therefore, deducting the water from each, we find that 85.8 parts of dry rice gave 76.4 parts of dry koji, equal to 89%, or in other words, 11% of material was lost by the dry rice. This loss is probably nearly all starch, and if so, every 100 parts of rice converted into koji would evolve nearly 18 parts of carbonic acid. Now 107 pounds of dry rice are converted into koji every day in each chamber, and thus evolve 19.2 pounds of carbonic acid measuring 2240 liters. The total capacity of each chamber cannot be more than 20,000 liters, and therefore in order to remove the carbonic acid formed a constant circulation of air is necessary. If this were not provided for the air would not only become irrespirable by the workmen, but would also become unfit for the growth of the plant which requires a supply of oxygen. At the same time care has to be taken that the current of fresh air is not sufficiently rapid to lower the temperature of the air within the chamber. The mode of ventilation depends upon the difference in temperature between the inner and the outer air, the inner air being warmer rises up a square shaft at the front end of the series of passages, whilst the cold air bringing fresh oxygen enters and flows along the floors of the chambers, until in its turn it is warmed and rises through the shaft to the air above. This method is amply sufficient during winter when the difference of temperature between the air outside and inside is about 40°F, but when, as in the spring and early summer the difference becomes less than 10°F, frequent stoppages occur. This, perhaps, might be remedied by burning a small fire at the foot of the shaft, and thus artificially causing a draft, but as a smaller quantity of koji is required in summer, it is not of so much importance.

In the germination of barley Day[*] has shown that an amount of oxygen is absorbed by the grain greater than is required to produce the carbonic acid liberated and he concludes that this increased absorption of oxygen is not connected with the liberation of carbonic acid. Whether a similar absorption occurs in the present case is not known, but if, as is not improbably, it does occur, the amount of starchy material lost by the rice during the conversion into koji will be even greater than that given above. The amount of carbon oxidized during the germination of the barley grain is said by Day to be about 2.5 percent., and he finds that there is a pretty constant relation between the carbon oxidized and the water formed, which averages 12 carbon to 18.28 water. Thus for every atom of carbon oxidized one molecule of water is liberated, a ratio which would agree with the formula for dextrose $C_6H_{12}O_6$ or in its simplest form CH_2O. Possibly a similar relation may be observed in the case of koji; that a large liberation of water does occur is evidenced by the increased percentage contained by the koji compared with that in the rice, and also by the moisture of the atmosphere in the chamber. If however, a fixed relation were to exist it would be hidden owing to the moistening of the rice which takes place on the second day; in the instance just discussed the ratio between the weight of carbon burnt and water contained by the koji in excess of that contained in the rice at starting is very nearly 12:24 or 3 atoms of carbon to 4 molecules of water; an amount of water greater than corresponds to the formula for dextrose.

---

[*] Mittheilungen der deutschen Gesselschaft fur Natur and Volkerkuneostasiens. 16tes. Heft. 1878.

[*] Journal Chem. Soc. 1880 Trans. p. 650.

Chapter 3. Active Properties

In the presentation of sake the koji is added to the steamed rice and water, and the solution, mixed with the insoluble residue of starch and cellulose, then acts upon the steamed rice. To study this action more readily it is more convenient to make use of a filtered aqueous extract of koji, for it has been ascertained that the active property of the koji, the "diastase", is dissolved out by contact with water. And first as to the nature of the solution. A sample of koji when powdered or rubbed down in a porcelain mortar and then digested with water for a short time gives, after filtration, a yellow liquid which contains dextrin, dextrose, albumenoid matter, and a small quantity of mineral matter. The proportions which the three first of these constituents bear to one another depend upon two things: 1.) The quantity of water used in proportion to the koji. 2) The duration of the digestion, whilst 3) the temperature at which the digestion is effected affects the amount of the total matter dissolved and the rapidity with which it enters into solution. Table 9 gives the results of experiments made at the ordinary temperature of the air, showing the truth of the first two of these statements.

In column II the volume of water used to dissolve the soluble matter of 100 grams of koji is given; in III, the time during which the water and the koji remained in contact; in IV, the number of grams of solid matter dissolved from 100 grams of koji by the amount of water mentioned; column V gives the average percentage of solid matter in the experiments indicated; column VI gives the percentage of dextrose contained in the solid matter; column VII, the specific rotatory power of the solution, and VIII, the average specific rotatory power of the solutions indicated. In experiments 2 to 12 the amount of water used for 100 grams of koji was 1000 c.c. and these experiments include three differing periods of digestion, but there is no evidence that the time of digestion has much influence upon the quantity of matter dissolved, at least at the temperature 10–15° C. The average percentage of solid matter dissolved is 27.0. Experiments 14 to 17 show how much solid matter is dissolved when the amount of water used is 2500 c.c. to 100 grams of koji; the average percentage being 31.4. We see, therefore, that when a larger quantity of water is used the amount of solid matter obtained in solution is greater. It is not possible to draw any definite conclusions from single experiments, but the very large percentage dissolved when 100 grams of koji were digested with 10,000 c.c. of water, bears out the above observations.

Table 9: Amount of Solid Matter Dissolved by Water from 100 grams of Koji at 10–15°C.

I	II	III	IV	V	VI	VII	VIII
Number	Volume of water used	Time	Weight of solid matter in solution	Avg. weight of solids	Percent dextrose in solid matter	Specific rotatory power	Avg. specific rotatory power
1	500 cc	12 hours	17.7		60.0	65°	
2	1000	18	25.7			61	
3	"	"	24.2			55.7	57.6
4	"	"	23.0			56.0	
5	"	12	33.3		49.0	65.3	
6	"	"	33.3		50.9	65.4	
7	"	"	29.4	27.0	45.0	62.9	
8	"	"	28.6		46.5	67.7	64.6
9	"	"	26.8		53.0	61.4	
10	"	"	22.5		53.0	64.5	
11	"	"	22.2		54.0	65.0	
12	"	4	28.0			61.4	
13	2000	3	31.1		68.0	78.0	
14	2500	"	32.2		58.0	68.1	
15	"	"	32.5	31.4	70.0	65.2	69.3
16	"	"	30.7		65.0	73.8	
17	"	"	30.1		68.0	70.2	
18	5000	24	30.0		47.0	64.5	
19	10000	"	40.0		66.0	60.5	

We have next to consider the influence of time upon the nature of the soluble matter. We have seen that it does not after 3 or 4 hours at the ordinary temperature affect very much the total amount of solids dissolved. But column VIII, which gives the average specific rotatory power of three series of experiments lasting respectively 18, 12, and 3 hours, shows that at 18 hours the specific rotatory power is smaller than at 12 hours, and at 12 hours less than at 3 hours. What is the meaning of this variation? The specific rotatory power of the solution is made up of three factors. The specific rotatory power of dextrin is 216°, that of dextrose is 59°. If these were the only two substances present the specific rotatory power of the solution would lie between these two numbers having a value proportionate to the amount of each present. It will be seen however, that the average of the experiments at 18 hours is less than 59°, and this shows that something else is present which tends to lower the value of the specific rotatory power. The albumenoids which are held in solution have been ascertained by nitrogen determinations to have an average value of –40°, and it is owing to their presence that the specific rotatory power is so low as it is. The composition of the liquid in experiment 6, for example, will illustrate this more clearly. 100 c.c. of the solution contained 1.695 gram dextrose, 0.723 gram dextrin, and 0.914 of albumenoids (calculated by multiplying the nitrogen found by 6.3). This gives a composition in 100 parts shown in the table below.

Dextrose	50.9%
Dextrin	21.7%
Albumenoids	27.4%
	100%

The observed specific rotatory power was 65.4°. The calculated specific power was obtained in the following way:

$$(0.509 \times 59) + (0.217 \times 216) + (0.274 - 40) = 30.031 + 46.872 \; 10.96 = 65.94$$

The calculated number thus agrees very well with the observed number and we may, therefore, assume the specific rotatory power of the albumenoids to be expressed by the number –40°.

Taking the series of experiments which lasted for 3 hours we find that the average specific rotatory power is 69.3°, about 10° higher than that of pure dextrose; the average specific rotatory power of those at 12 hours is 64.6°, about 5° higher than that of dextrose, and that of the experiments at 18 hours 57.6°, about 1.4° lower than that of pure dextrose. This diminution occurs because the amount of albumenoids in solution is greater when the specific rotatory power is less, their left handed rotation partially neutralizing the right handed rotation of the dextrin and dextrose. But why is it that the amount of albumenoids is greater when the treatment with water is longer continued? The most probable explanation is that as the albumenoids exist in the koji, they are not entirely soluble; a portion is already soluble in water, but the rest is only brought into solution by the action of the water itself, and perhaps also, through the agency of the albumenoids at first dissolved. It is in fact a chemical reaction which takes time for its completion, and probably, if sufficient time were allowed, the whole of the nitrogenous matter of the rice would be degraded and brought into solution. This is a point of importance to brewers of sake, for we shall see that the power which the koji possesses of transforming rice into dextrose, capable of undergoing alcoholic fermentation, is due to the presence of these albumenoids in solution.

The effect of heating a mixture of koji and water is to bring the matter into solution much more rapidly than at a low temperature.

Table 10: Action of Water at Higher Temperatures Upon 100 grams of Koji

Exp.	Time and Temperature	c.c. of water / 100 gr. koji	Solid matter dissolved	Dextrose % or solids	Specific rot. power
1	2 hours at 50° + 18 hours at 15° C.	1700	51.80	68.0	68°
2	1/2 hour at 45° C.	2000	31.80	84.9	76.1°
3	2 hours at 45° C.	2000	61.6	68.5	58.5°
4	1/2 hour at 50° C.	5000	37.2	66.0	63.2°
5	24 hours at 15° + 2 hours at 100°	10000	49.2	58.0	73.8°

With the exception of Experiment 2, the percentage of matter dissolved by the water is greater than in the experiments conducted at a lower temperature, and as a rule the percentage of dextrose in the solid matter is also greater. We shall, however, learn something by comparing experiments 2 and 3 with an experiment made at the ordinary temperature with the same sample of koji. In every respect the conditions of the three experiments were the same except as regards time and temperature.

Table 11: Action of Water on Koji

Exp.	Time and Temperature	c.c. of water / 100 gr. koji	Solid matter dissolved	Dextrose % or solids	Specific rot. power
1	18 hours at 10–12° C.	2000	29.2	69.3	66.3°
2	1/2 hour at 45°	2000	31.8	84.9	76.1°
3	2 hours at 45°	2000	61.6	68.5	53.5°

The above comparison shows that the amount of solid matter dissolved when the contact between koji and water is for 18 hours at a low temperature and for 1/2 hour at a high temperature is very nearly the same, but the percentage of dextrose and the specific rotatory power of the solution indicate that the proportions in which the three ingredients are present are very different. If we assume the specific rotatory power of the albumenoids to be –40° we may ascertain the composition of the solid matter, and referring it to a fixed amount of dextrose we get per 100 parts of dextrose:

Table 12: Composition of Solid Matter per 100 Parts Dextrose

Exp.	Time and Temperature	Dextrin	Albumenoids
1	8 hours at 10–12° C.	21.2	23.10
2	1/2 hour at 45°	14.7	3.06
3	2 hours at 45°	14.6	25.30

After 18 hours at a low temperature the amount of dextrin is 21.2 parts for every 100 parts of dextrose, but after both 1/2 hour and 2 hours at 45°, it remains practically the same and about two-thirds of the amount in the former case. The most interesting fact to be observed is the variation in the amount of the albumenoids; after 18 hours at 10–12° C it is very little different from the amount dissolved out in 2 hours at a temperature of 45° C, but after only 1/2 hour at 45° C the quantity in solution is only about one-eighth as much as in the two other experiments. This bears out the observations made at lower temperatures viz. that the amount of albumenoid matter dissolved is mainly affected by the duration of the experiment. It is not only dependent upon that, for we see that influence of a higher temperature in dissolving the albumenoids more rapidly, 2 hours at 45° C being more than equivalent to 18 hours at 10–12°C. Thus we are again led to the conclusion that the greater part of the nitrogenous matter in koji is insoluble in water, but that it is in such a state that the prolonged contact with water renders it soluble.

Although the effect of heat upon the mixture of koji and water is thus marked, when the clear solution has been separated by filtration from the undissolved grains it is not so rapidly changed either by exposure to heat or by longer standing at the ordinary temperature of the air. It is important for us to examine the change in composition of the solution on heating, as in the experiments upon starch-paste to be presently described it is the filtered solution of koji which is used. Table 13 gives the results of a number of experiments made by Watanabe Yuzuruy, graduate, on the effect of heating filtered solutions of koji for one hour at the specified temperatures, the same solution being examined for comparison after standing at the ordinary temperature for the same time.

Below 45° C the change in the composition of the liquid is so small that it may practically be neglected, but between 45°C and 60°C the effect is much more marked. An increase in the amount of solid matter and in the dextrose occurs, accompanied by a decrease in the specific rotatory power. These results are caused by an absorption of water by the dextrin which is converted into dextrose and thus the amount of solid matter in a given volume of the liquid is increased which, together with the smaller specific rotatory power of the dextrose, lowers the specific rotatory power of the solution.

Table 13: Action of Heat on Filtered Solutions of Koji

Temp.	Solids in 100 c.c. of solution			Dextrose in 100 c.c. of solution			Specific rotatory power		
	Unheated	Heated	Increase	Unheated	Heated	Increase	Unheated	Heated	Increase
30° C.	4.88	-	-	2.97	3.015	0.045	-	-	-
35°	4.88	-	-	2.97	3.062	0.092	-	-	-
40°	4.89	-	-	2.98	3.079	0.099	-	-	-
45°	4.92	4.98	0.06	2.92	3.412	0.494	74.0°	70°	4°
50°	4.95	5.02	0.07	2.793	3.285	0.492	70°	67.1°	2.9°
55°	4.92	5.00	0.08	2.918	3.463	0.545	74°	68.9°	5.1°
60°	4.95	5.02	0.07	2.793	3.30	0.507	70°	67.8°	2.2°
65°	4.89	-	-	2.98	3.081	0.101	-	-	-
70°	4.89	-	-	2.98	3.075	0.095	-	-	-

The alteration is greatest at the temperature of 55° C, above which it rapidly diminishes. At 65° C and at 70° the effect produced is very much the same as at ordinary temperatures, so far as the composition of the liquid itself is concerned, but a very great change in the active properties of the liquid is brought about by heating it to these temperatures. The liquid becomes turbid, so much so that its specific rotatory power cannot be determined with any accuracy, an effect caused by the precipitation of a certain proportion of the albumenoids which have been rendered insoluble by heating. We shall see that at some temperature between 60°C and 70°C the liquid loses its power of transforming starch into sugar, and reasons will appear connecting this loss of activity with the precipitation of the albumenoids.

Chapter 4. Action of Koji Extract Upon Some Carbohydrates

The solution which is prepared by digesting koji in water possesses certain active properties which cause it to resemble in general character the aqueous solution of malt, so carefully experimented upon by Messrs. Brown and Heron. It is of interest and importance to compare the action of koji extract upon the principal carbohydrates in order to establish an identity or a difference between the two species of diastase. From the mode of production there is no reason to suppose that they will be found to be identical, and experiments to be hereafter described will prove that, though they agree in some points, they differ in yet others. The carbohydrates which have been subjected to the action of koji extract are cane-sugar, maltose, dextrin, and gelatinized starch.

Brown and Heron have shown that when an aqueous solution of malt is allowed to remain in contact with a solution of cane sugar, a change takes place by which the cane sugar is made to take up water and is thereby converted into invert sugar, a mixture of dextrose and levulose. The diastase of malt is said by them to exert its maximum effect upon sugar at 55°C; its action is considerably weakened at 60°C and almost destroyed at 66°C.

Experiment shows that the extract of koji also possesses the property of causing cane sugar to become inverted, but I am not able to define the limits of its action. The following experiments will suffice to prove this point.

Experiment 1: 1.974 gram of dry cane sugar was dissolved in 25 cc of koji extract, then diluted with water to 100 cc. The amount of rotation was found to be 15.8 divisions, and the calculated number 15.5 divisions.

1.974 grams case sugar dissolved in 100 c.c. gives rotation	= 12.1 div.
25 c.c. koji solution diluted to 100 c.c. gives rotation	= 3.4
	15.5 div.

After being allowed to stand for 18 hours at about 10 to 12°C the rotation was found to have diminished to 5 divisions, and the solution contained 1.67 grams of glucose. Deducting 0.36 gram contained in 25 cc of koji solution, the amount, formed from the cane sugar was 1.31 gram, equivalent to 1.2445 gram cane sugar and hence 0.7294 gram of unaltered cane sugar was present. We thus find the calculated number of divisions rotated by the inverted solution to be +5.43 against 5 divisions actually observed.

Unaltered cane sugar (0.7294 grams in 100 c.c.)	+4.4 div.
Koji extract (25 c.c.) in 100 c.c. of water)	+3.4 div
Invert sugar formed	–2.37 div.
	+5.43 div

Calculated in degrees of arc the specific rotatory power of the can sugar has been reduced from 74° to 10°.

Experiment 2: A solution of case sugar containing 5.41 grams in 100 cc, and giving a rotation in a 200 mm tube of 33.1 divisions, equal to [a] = 74°, was employed. 75 cc of this solution was mixed with 25 cc of a solution of koji which contained in 100 cc 1.46 gram of solid matter, 1.0125 gram of glucose, and which gave in a 200 mm tube an optical rotation of 8 divisions. It may be remarked that from this and other experiments made with the same solution of koji, it was found to be exceptionally weak in its converting power. The observations are as follow, after deducting the optical rotation due to the presence of the koji solution:

	Optical rotation	Specific rotatory power
At starting	24.8 div.	74°
After 1-1/2 hours at 15°C	23.7	70.6
After 20-1/4 hours at 10–12°	21.0	62.6
After 3/4 hour more at 40°C	20.2	60.2

50 cc of this mixture and 25 cc of koji were treated as below. The numbers given are corrected for the koji present:

	Optical rotation	Specific rotatory power
After 1-1/4 hours at 40°C	11.2 div.	50°
After 2 hours at 45-50°	4.0	17.8

The experiment was not carried further than this. At low temperature the converting action of this particular extract of koji is very slow, but at higher temperatures, and especially at from 45° to 50°C it is much more rapid. In this respect, therefore, koji extract resembles malt extract.

Action Upon Maltose

So recently as 1872 Mr. O'Sullivan* directed attention to the nature of the sugar formed when malt extract is made to act upon gelatinized starch, and his experiments conclusively established the existence of a new sugar, previously, however, pointed out by Dubrunfaut, which is now known as *maltose*. In composition it agrees with cane sugar, but differs from it in having a specific rotatory power of 150°, and in forming dextrose and not invert sugar when boiled with acids or otherwise hydrated. It also differs in its reducing action upon oxide of copper from either cane sugar or dextrose, for the former has no reducing action upon cupric oxide, while maltose reduces only 61 to 63% of the amount reduced by the same weight of dextrose. Messrs. Brown and Heron‡ have shown that a solution of malt is not able to convert maltose into dextrose, and that it is quite without action upon it. The following experiments will, however, show that the solution of koji possesses the property of hydrating maltose and converting it into dextrose. This will be rendered evident by the change which the solution of maltose undergoes under the influence of koji extract both as regards the weight of oxide of copper reduced by a given weight of the solid, and as regards the specific rotatory power of the product.

The maltose employed was obtained from *ame*, a kind of sweetmeat prepared by the action of malt in solution upon the starch contained in millet or in rice. Various specimens of *ame* contained from 68 to 94% maltose, which was separated according to the process described by O'Sullivan*. The specimens employed were in the crystalline state, and contained water sufficient to reduce the specific rotatory power from 150° to 144.5°.

Table 14: Action of Koji on Maltose

Time	Solids in 500 cc after deducting koji	Rotation after deducting koji	Specific rot. power of maltose prods.
10 minutes	2.826	5.8 div.	124.2°
30 minutes		5.3	111.1
1 hour	2.886	4.7	98.5
2 hours		3.7	77.6

The specific rotatory power therefore, fell from 144.5° to 77.6° in 2 hours, and would doubtless have fallen to 59° if the solution had not been used up after 2 hours. The action may be represented in the form of a curve using time and specific rotatory power as abscisse and ordinates respectively (See Figure 3).

The curve shows very clearly how regular the action is, and leaves no doubt about the power of extract of koji to effect the hydration of maltose. It is especially important to establish this, because this property marks in the sharpest manner the difference between malt extract and koji extract. Brown and Heron's experiments leave no doubt about the inability of malt extract to convert maltose into dextrose, and these experiments, I think, establish conclusively the ability of koji extract to do this.

Action Upon Dextrin

The action of koji upon dextrin is to cause it slowly to combine with water and form dextrose, as the following experiment shows.

Experiment 6: 100 cc of a solution of commercial dextrin containing 5.56 grams of solid matter were diluted to 250 cc and then gave a specific rotatory power $[a]j = 174°$. It was, therefore, impure, and contained a considerable percentage of dextrose.

Figure 3: Curve showing action of koji on maltose

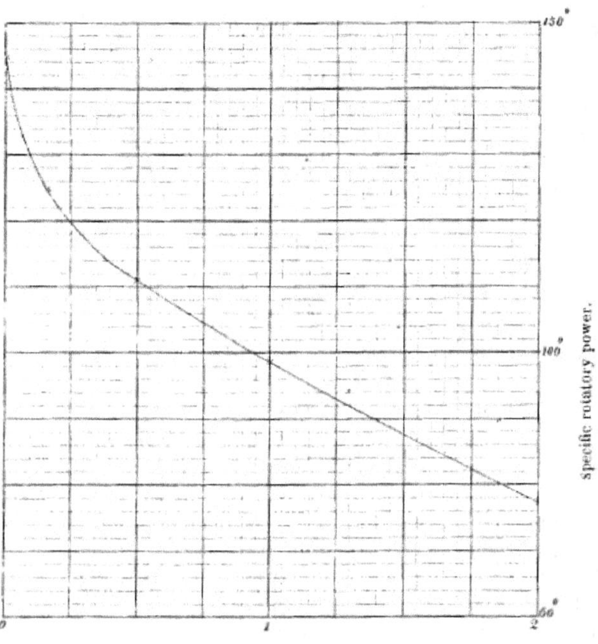

50 c.c. of this solution were mixed with 50 c.c. of a solution of koji and heated to 45°C for 1-1/2 hour. After being diluted to 250 c.c. the solution contained 4.145 grams of solid matter in 250 c.c., and deducting 1.285 gram contained in the 50 cc of koji solution added, we get 2.86 grams of solids formed from the 50 c.c. of dextrin solution, instead of 2.78 grams originally present. After making allowance for the rotation caused by the koji solution, the specific rotatory power of the dextrin products was 92°, instead of 174° that of the substance at starting. The koji solution had become exhausted, because when an additional amount of koji solution was added, and the mixture heated for a longer time, the specific rotatory power further diminished to 85°. This experiment leaves no doubt concerning the gradual absorption of water by dextrin under the solution of koji.

---

[*] Journ. Chem. Soc 1872, p. 579.

‡ Jour. Chem. Soc. 1879. Trans., p. 621.

* Journ. Chem. Soc. 1876, ii, p. 127.

Chapter 5. Action of Koji Extract Upon Gelatinized Starch

From the point of view of the sake brewer, the change which koji solution produces in the nature of starch is of the utmost importance, and it will on that account be needful to enter into somewhat minute details concerning its action under varying conditions of time and temperature. That a remarkable change does take place will be evident to any one who adds a few cubic centimeters of a filtered solution of koji to a quantity of thick starch paste, especially if the latter be at a temperature of about 45° to 50° C. Within a very short time, a few minutes at most, the paste or jelly which before would not have moved on inverting the vessel containing it, will become as liquid as water, and if the flocks of cellulose be allowed to settle, as transparent as water. This cannot be observed in the ordinary process of manufacture, but the change takes place, it is only disguised by the presence of a considerable quantity of insoluble matter. In order, therefore, to understand the chemical reactions involved in sake brewing, the first point is to ascertain the composition of the clear, transparent solution obtained as above described.

Using malt extract instead of koji extract a similar change would be observed, and the nature of the resulting solution has been very thoroughly examined by O'Sullivan*, and more recently by Brown and Heron‡. The result of their investigations has been to prove that dextrin and maltose are the only products of the solution of starch by malt extract, and that the change may be represented by definite chemical equations, which are different according to the temperature at which the conversion takes place. Thus according to O'Sullivan when the malt solution is allowed to act upon gelatinized starch at the ordinary temperature of the air, or at any temperature whatever below 63°C, the reaction is presented by his equation A.

A
$$6\,(C^{12}H_{20}O_{10}) + 4\,H_2O = 4\,C^{12}H_{22}O_{11} + 2\,C^{12}H_{20}O_{10}$$

Soluble starch   Maltose   β-dextrin iii

That is to say that the products of the reaction contain 67.8% of maltose and 32.2% of dextrin, and have a specific rotatory power of 170.6°.

Between the temperatures 64° and 66°C, the reaction is represented by the B′ equation.

B′
$$6\,(C^{12}H_{20}O_{10}) + 3\,H2O = 3\,C^{12}H_{22}O_{11} + 3\,C^{12}H_{20}O_{10}$$

Soluble starch   Maltose   β-dextrin ii

Between 67°C and 70°C, equation B represents the reaction.

B
$$6\,(C^{12}H_{20}O_{10}) + 2\,H2O = 2\,C^{12}H_{22}O_{11} + 4\,C^{12}H_{20}O_{10}$$

Soluble starch Maltose B-dextrin i

Between 70°C and the point at which the activity of the malt diastase is destroyed, the reaction is expressed by equation C.

C
$$6\,(C^{12}H_{20}O_{10}) + H2O = C^{12}H_{22}O_{11} + 5\,C^{12}H_{20}O_{10}$$

Soluble starch Maltose α-dextrin

Brown and Heron agree with O'Sullivan in finding only maltose and dextrin as the products of the action of malt extract upon starch, but their experiments lead them to represent the proportions formed at different temperatures a little differently. There is also a difference in their theoretic views as to the weight of the molecule of soluble starch and the nature of the dextrins, but we may leave that aside. They imagine that the conversion of starch into maltose and dextrin is to be represented by nine difference equations in the following manner:

1 $\quad 10\,(C^{12}H_{20}O_{10}) + H_{2}O = C^{12}H_{22}O_{11} + 9\,C^{12}H_{20}O_{10}$ (Erythro-dextrin α)

2 $\quad 10\,(C^{12}H_{20}O_{10}) + 2\,H_{2}O = 2\,C^{12}H_{22}O_{11} + 8\,C^{12}H_{20}O_{10}$ (Erythro-dextrin B)

3 $\quad 10\,(C^{12}H_{20}O_{10}) + 3\,H_{2}O = 3\,C^{12}H_{22}O_{11} + 7\,C^{12}H_{20}O_{10}$ (Achroo-dextrin α)

4 $\quad 10\,(C^{12}H_{20}O_{10}) + 4\,H_{2}O = 4\,C^{12}H_{22}O_{11} + 6\,C^{12}H_{20}O_{10}$ (Achroo-dextrin B)

The series is continued through the intermediate equations.

8 $\quad 10\,(C^{12}H_{20}O_{10}) + 8\,H_{2}O = 8\,C^{12}H_{22}O_{11} + 2\,C^{12}H_{20}O_{10}$ (Achroo-dextrin ζ)

9 $\quad 10\,(C^{12}H_{20}O_{10}) + 9\,H_{2}O = 9\,C^{12}H_{22}O_{11} + C^{12}H_{20}O_{10}$ (Achroo-dextrin η)

Of these, the most stable is number 8 which represents the manner in which the reaction takes place at and below 63°C. They consider also that they have definite evidence of the existence of equations 4, 3, and 2, and indications of 5 and 6.

It will be seen that the weight of maltose formed at low temperatures is always greater than at high temperatures, a circumstance which has to be carefully attended to in the process of making beer, because it depends upon the proportion of sugar in the wort whether the brewed liquid will contain much or little alcohol.

The above mentioned observers have been able to obtain definite chemical equations because of the absence of any hydrating action of malt extract upon maltose. As, however, it has been shown in Chapter 4 that the solution of koji hydrates maltose, we cannot expect, even if that sugar is formed, to obtain results of the same sharpness as where the products first formed are unacted upon.

We have, therefore, in the first place to ascertain whether maltose is one of the products of the action of koji extract upon starch paste, and that it is so, will be shown by the following experiments.

To prove this an indirect method is resorted to, on account of the difficulty of isolating small quantities of maltose in a pure state from solutions containing much dextrin. The method adopted consists in determining the reducing action of the solution upon oxide of copper, and from the amount of cuprous oxide precipitated by a given weight of the starch products in solution (calculated from the specific gravity of the liquid) to find the weights of maltose and dextrin, assuming these to be the products. If no other substance is formed, the specific rotatory power of the solution calculated from the percentages of maltose and dextrin present will agree with the specific rotatory power of the solution actually observed. If they do agree the solution must contain the bodies assumed to be present, because if others were there, the specific rotatory powers would differ from one another. A detailed description of one experiment will render this more intelligible.

Experiment 7: A koji solution was prepared by digesting for a short time 25 grams of freshly prepared sample of koji in about 100 cc of water. The liquid was then filtered, the residue digested with a fresh quantity of water, and the whole thrown upon the filter and washed until the filtrate amounted nearly to 500 cc. The solution was then diluted exactly to 500 cc at 15°C. The filtration occupied three or four hours even with the assistance of a filter pump on account of the slimy nature of the insoluble matter. The solution so made contained in 100 cc 1.46 gram of solid matter calculated from the specific gravity (using the divisor 3.86), 1.0125 gram glucose, and caused an optical rotation of 8 divisions in a 200 mm tube. This gives a specific rotatory power:

$$[a]_j = \frac{8 \times 0.242}{2 \times 0.0146} = 66.3°$$

5 grams of starch, previously dried at 100°C, were gelatinized with about 75 cc of water, the paste allowed to cool to 40°C, then mixed with 25 cc of the koji solution, and left for 25

minutes till it was quite clear. It was then rapidly heated to boiling, cooled, and diluted to 250 cc. 100 cc of this solution, after filtration, contained 2.15 grams of solid matter, and 0.63 gram glucose, determined by weighing the reduced cuprous oxide after ignition. The optical rotation in a 200 mm tube was 32.4 divisions.

As the koji solution contained in 250 cc of the starch products was 25 cc (i.e., one tenth) we must deduct the weight of solid matter and glucose contained in 10 cc of the koji extract from the weights above found in 100 cc of the liquid. The optical rotation must also be diminished by one tenth the amount caused by the koji solution alone. We thus get:

Solids in 100 cc formed from starch	2.15 − 0.146	= 2.004 grams
Sugar, calculated as glucose	0.63 − 0.101	= 0.529 gram
Optical rotation	32.4 − 0.8	= 31.6 divisions

$$\text{Thus } [a]_j \text{observed} = \frac{31.6 \times 0.242}{2 \times 0.02004} = 190.8°$$

The percentage of sugar calculated as glucose is 26.39, and the maltose corresponding is 26.39 / 0.61 = 43.28%, and the dextrin, therefore, 100 − 43.28 = 56.72. If we calculate the specific rotatory power which a mixture of maltose and dextrin in these proportions ought to have we find it to be: $[a]_j$ calculated = 216 x 0.567 + 150 x 0.433 = 187.4°

There is a difference between the two results of 3.4°, which is not more than might be caused by errors of experiment. If we assumed the solution to contain dextrin and dextrose, the specific rotatory power would be only 174°, a difference of nearly 17°. This experiment, therefore, shows that maltose and not dextrose, is formed.

Experiment 8: 5 grams of starch were gelatinized and after cooling to 40°C mixed with 25 cc of the same koji extract and kept at that temperature for 3/4 hour. An additional 25 cc of koji was then added and the whole allowed to remain at 40°C for 15 minutes longer, then boiled and diluted to 250 cc. After filtration the solution contained, deduction having been made for the koji added:

Solid matter	2.035 grams in 100 cc
Sugar (calculated as dextrose)	0.888 grams in 100 cc
Optical rotation	28.5 divisions
Hence $[a]_j$ observed	169.5°

The composition of the solution, assuming the sugar to be maltose is:

Maltose	71.54 %
Dextrin	28.46 %
	100.0%

The specific rotatory power calculated for this mixture is 168.8°, which agrees very closely with the observed number.

Experiment 9: With a solution prepared from different koji, using 50 cc of the koji solution containing 1.206 gram of solid matter per 100 cc, the following results were obtained from 5 grams of gelatinized starch kept for 2 hours at 10–15°C.

Maltose	70.0 %
Dextrin	30.0 %
	100.0%

Specific rotatory power observed is 174.0°.

Specific rotatory power calculated is 169.8°.

The two last experiments give results which correspond nearly with Brown and Heron's equation number 7:

$$10 \, (C^{12}H_{20}O_{10}) + 7 \, H_2O = 7 \, C^{12}H_{22}O_{11} + 3 \, C^{12}H_{20}O_{10}$$

which requires 70.9 % of maltose and [*a*]j calculated = 169.2°.

Solutions in which maltose can be detected can only be obtained by making use of dilute solutions of koji and in comparatively small quantity. In by far the greater number of experiments the maltose which is at first formed is hydrated to dextrose by the excess of diastase present in the koji solution and as in the brewing operations a very large excess of koji is used, the brewer of sake has practically nothing to do with maltose, but only with dextrose. In this respect the brewing process in Japan differs from beer brewing in Europe and America, where the alcohol is fermented for the most part from maltose.

The following experiments will serve to illustrate the production of dextrose and dextrin only. The mode of recognizing the nature of the products is the same in principle as that used to identify maltose vis a comparison of the observed specific rotatory power with the number calculated from the percentages of sugar and dextrin, assuming in this case the sugar to be dextrose with a specific rotatory power [*a*]j = 59°.

Experiment 10: 20 grams of dry starch gelatinized and 200 cc of a solution of koji (prepared from 50 grams in 500 cc of water) diluted to one liter were heated to 30°C for 6 hours, then allowed to stand for 2 hours at 15°C. The solution contained in 100 cc (deduction having been made for the koji extract) 1.96 gram of solid matter and 1.68 gram glu cose, with a rotation of 12.8 divisions. This gives:

Dextrose	85.7 %
Dextrin	14.3 %
	100.0%

Specific rotatory power observed is 79.0°.

Specific rotatory power calculated is 81.4°.

Experiment 11: 4 grams of gelatinized starch and 96 cc of koji solution (20 grams of koji in 500 cc of water) were heated at 45°C for 3-1/2 hours, then evaporated to about 200 cc and diluted to 250 cc. The composition of the solid matter in solution, after deducting the koji extract, was:

Dextrose	86.0 %
Dextrin	14.0 %
	100.0%

Specific rotatory power observed is 85.7°.

Specific rotatory power calculated is 81°.

In both experiments, therefore, dextrin and dextrose are the only products.

Experiments were next directed towards ascertaining the degree of rapidity with which the conversion of starch into dextrose took place at different temperatures. For this purpose it was necessary to allow the mixture of starch and koji solution to react for some time, and to ascertain the composition of the solution, or its specific rotatory power, at different stages. Setting out in one direction the duration of the digestion, and in a direction at right angles to this the specific rotatory power of the solution at stated intervals, the progress of the action can be represented by a curved line, using the specific rotatory power as a measure of the change which has occurred in a given time.

The first series of experiments was carried out at the temperature of the air, which at that time varied between 4° and 10°C.

Experiment 12: 450 cc of starch paste containing 11.43 grams of dry starch were mixed with 50 cc of koji extract. The whole was allowed to stand at this temperature with an occasional shaking and samples were withdrawn after 48, 120, 192, and 240 hours, respectively. After making a deduction for the 50 cc of koji solution used, the amount of solids in 500 cc and the optical rotation were found to be as follow:

Table 15: Action of Koji on Starch at 4–10°C

Time	Total starch in solution (koji deducted)	Specific rotatory power of starch
48 hours	9.714 grams	109.6°
120 hours	9.904 grams	100.2°
192 hours	10.369 grams	90.4°
240 hours	10.450 grams	80.4°

The curve illustrating this series of experiments is seen in Figure 4. The action upon the starch, as indicated by the fall in the specific rotatory power, is more rapid at the beginning of the experiment, but afterwards proceeds in a regular and continuous manner during the remainder of the experiment.

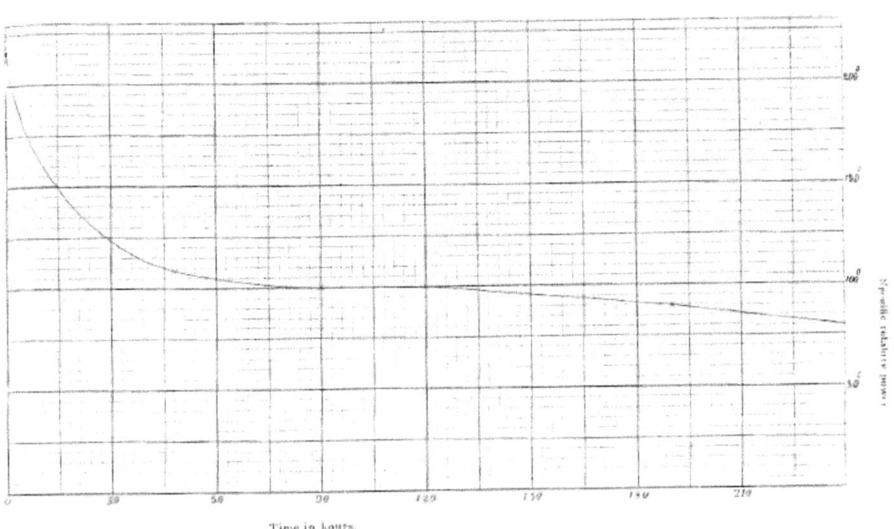

The second set of experiments was conducted at the same temperature, different proportions of koji and starch being used. The amounts of koji and starch used for the following table were 5 grams of starch to 20 grams of koji.

Table 16: Action of Koji on Starch at 4–10°C

Time	Total starch in solution (koji deducted)	Specific rotatory power of starch
48 hours	4.638 grams	100.4°
164 hours	4.816 grams	75.3°

In this series the same specific rotatory power, 100.4° is attained in 68 hours, which it took 120 hours in the former series to arrive at, and the reduction is greater in the last series in 164 hours, than in 240 hours of the former. The reason of this lies in the larger proportion of koji used in the second than in the first series of experiments, but although four times as much koji was used, the rapidity of the action appears to be only about twice as great.

The third and fourth series of experiments were made at a temperature varying between 10° and 15°C, but otherwise they were conducted as before.

Table 17: Action of Koji on Starch at 10–15°C

Time	Total starch in solution (koji deducted)	Specific rotatory power of starch
1/2 hour	10.61 grams	172.8°
2 hours	10.45	158
21-1/2	10.56	131
26	10.65	120.4
46	10.51	110.5

Table 18: Action of Koji on Starch at 10–15°C

Time	Total starch in solution (koji deducted)	Specific rotatory power of starch
1 hour	9.705 grams	-
48 hours	9.925	121°
72 hours	9.925	113

Figure 5 represents the first of these results in the form of a curve. It will be noticed that although the two series of experiments at 10–15°C were made to all appearance under exactly the same conditions, yet the reduction in the specific rotatory power at a given time is much greater in the second series. This may be accounted for in one of two ways. It may be that different portions even of the same preparation of koji differ in activity, or it may be that, although the limits of temperature in both cases were the same, the average temperature of the former series was higher than of the second set. That this might affect the results will be seen by reference to Figure 5 in which the inclination of the curve between 21-1/2 hours and 26 hours is greater than the average. This was undoubtedly the result of the solution during that interval having a higher temperature than the average of the whole time. These limits fell in the middle of the day when the temperature was 15° the whole time; if an examination of the liquid had not been made at the two periods mentioned this sudden drop would not have been observed, but the average inclination from the beginning to 21-1/2 hours would have appeared slightly greater. In the same way if the temperature had remained during one set of experiments more nearly 15° and in the other more nearly 10″ during the whole time, the action might be expected to be more rapid in the former than in the latter.

Figure 5: Curve showing action of koji extract on gelatinized starch at 10–15°C

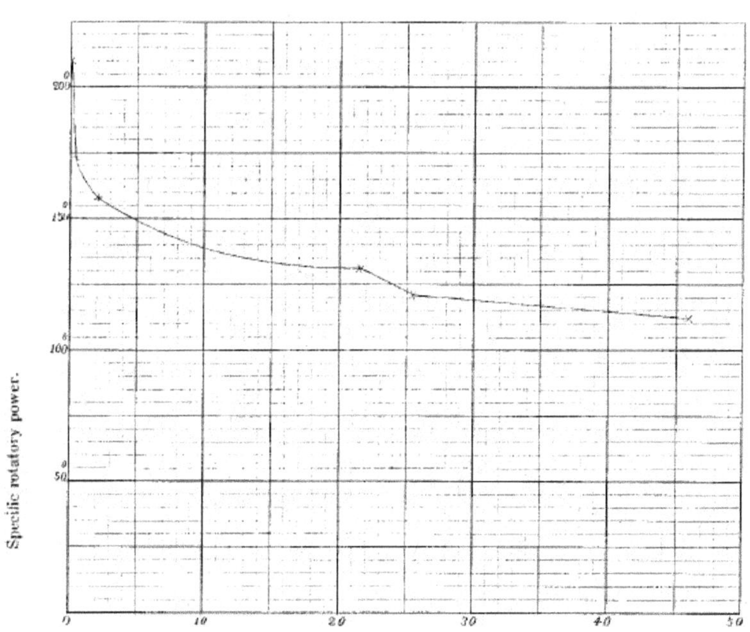

From these experiments we may understand what occurs during the mashing operations in sake making. At first they are conducted at even a lower temperature than 4°C, and this is interesting because it shows that the activity of the diastase in koji is not destroyed at low temperatures, even at 0°C.

At a higher temperature the reduction in the specific rotatory power of the solution goes on more rapidly, and although the sake brewer never uses temperatures so high as those of the succeeding experiments, it is of scientific interest to complete the record at all temperatures below that at which the diastase of koji is rendered inactive.

The experiments at higher temperatures were conducted in the following manner. The flask containing the mixture was immersed in a water bath and kept at the specified temperature, samples being taken at stated intervals. The portion used for determining the total solid matter in solution from its specific gravity was rapidly cooled by means of ice, and another portion in which the specific rotatory power was to be determined, was poured into a dry flask containing a little salicylic acid, as recommended by Brown and Heron*, and also rapidly cooled. Deduction was made for the amount of koji solution added as in the previous experiments.

The two next series of experiments were conducted at 40°C and only differ in the relative proportions of starch and koji used. The first series used 10 grams of starch to 5 grams of koji; the second used 10 grams of starch to 10 grams of koji.

Table 19: Action of koji on starch at 40°C

Time	Total starch in solution (koji deducted)	Specific rotatory power of starch
25 minutes	10.08 grams	167°
4 hours	10.08 grams	127°
> 92 hours at 15°C	10.25 grams	106°

Table 20: Action of koji on starch at 40°C

Time	Total starch in solution (koji deducted)	Specific rotatory power of starch
20 minutes	9.64 grams	143.1°
1 hour	9.64	127
2 hours	9.64	115
3 hours	9.65	105
4-1/2 hours	9.67	88
6 hours	9.69	86
> 20 hours at 15°C	9.79	80

In Figure 6 these results are represented in a graphic manner. The difference between the two sets lies in the fact that in the latter twice as much koji is used as in the former, and the result is that at any given time the diminution in the specific rotatory power is greater in the latter. Further, the general form of the two curves is similar and there is no evidence of any sudden break in the curve, such as in Brown and Heron's experiments indicates a definite chemical equation. Such a break could not be expected, seeing that the action of koji solution upon maltose would tend to disguise such reactions, by rubbing down the corners, as it were. Table 21 gives the results of a similar experiment made at 45°C.

Table 21: Action of koji on starch at 45°C

Time	Total starch in solution (koji deducted)	Specific rotatory power of starch
5 minutes	9.48 grams	142.6°
25 minutes	9.93	126.8
1 hour	9.93	106
1-1/2 hour	-	103.6
2 hours	9.98	103
3 hours	9.98	98.3
4 hours	-	98.3
1/5th more koji added		
4-1/2 hours	10.18	88

Figure 6: Curve showing action of koji extract on gelatinized starch at 40°C

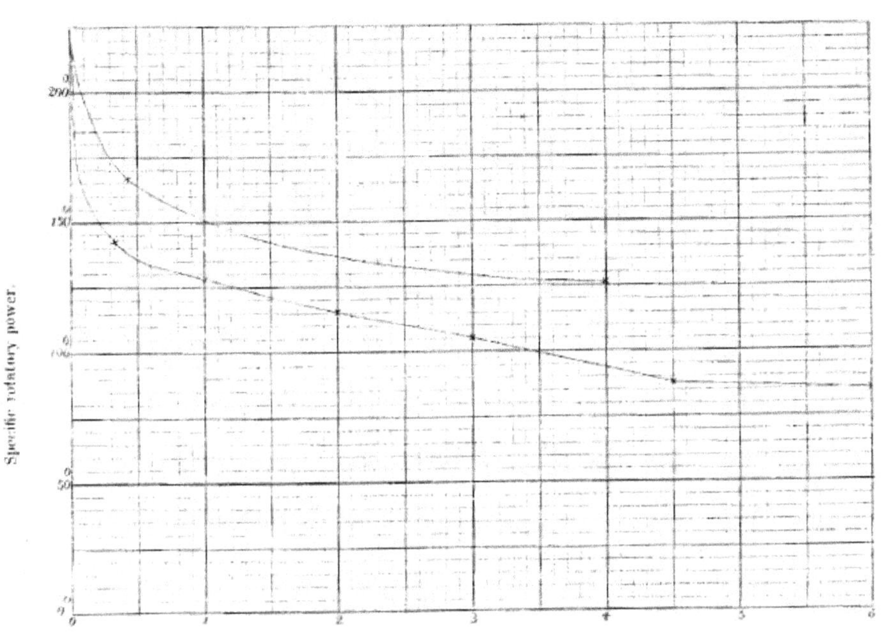

In the curve in Figure 7 which represents these results graphically, it will be noticed that during the first five minutes the fall in the specific rotatory power is very rapid until it arrives at $[a]j = 142.6°$ after which it proceeds very nearly a straight line until the specific rotatory power equals 106°, after which it remains almost the same, until after a fresh addition of koji, which causes a reduction to 88°. As the rate of reduction after the addition of a fresh quantity of koji is very nearly the same as at first, as is shown by the similarity in the inclinations of the curve, it is evident that the koji first added had been nearly exhausted when the specific rotatory power of 106° was attained.

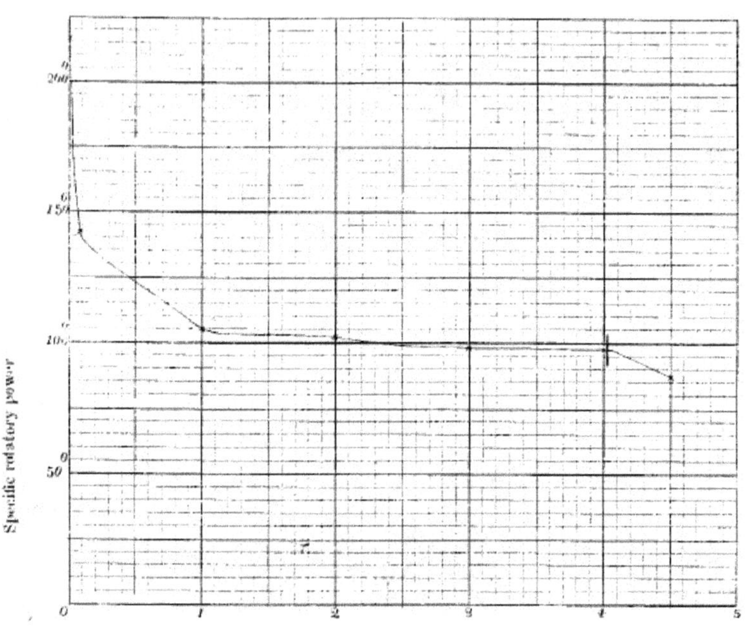

At a higher temperature, 60°C, the activity of the koji solution is very soon exhausted, as will be seen from the following results (Table 21), and from the curve in Figure 8. 10 grams of starch and 10 grams of koji were used.

The number found at 15 minutes is doubtless incorrect. After half an hour had elapsed, and the specific rotatory power had diminished to 168°, the action appeared to cease, until a fresh addition of koji was made, when it fell at a similar rate, and for nearly the same time as at first. The high temperature, therefore, very quickly renders the diastase of koji inactive.

At a temperature of 70°C practically no solution of starch took place from which it may be concluded that a temperature between 60° and 70°C renders it completely inert. The diastase of malt is not killed until between 80° and 81°, which constitutes another point of difference between the two. The two bodies resemble one another in this, that the loss of activity is accompanied by the appearance of a distinct precipitate, consisting of albumenoid matter that has been coagulated by heat. Messrs. Brown and Heron state that

Figure 8: Curve showing the action of koji extract on gelatinized starch at 60°C

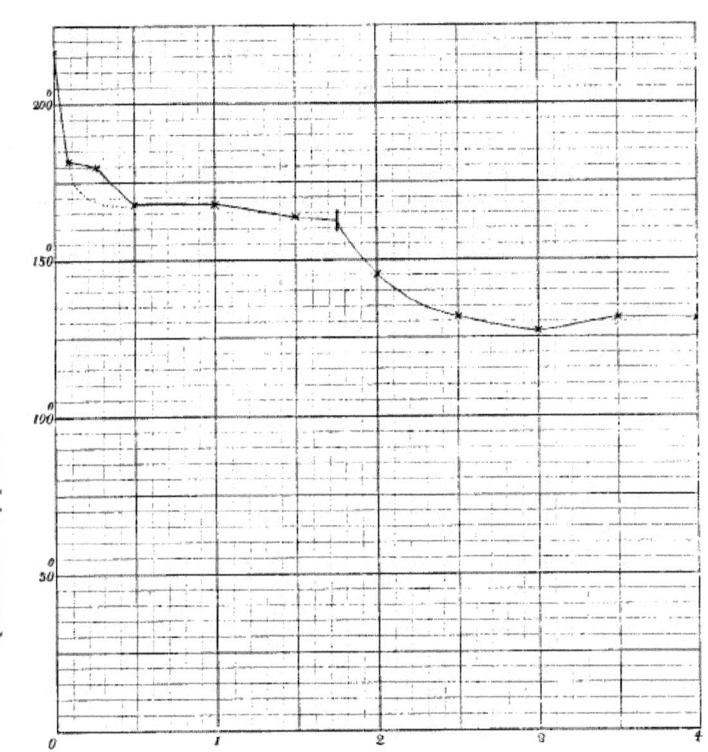

Time	Total starch in solution (koji deducted)	Specific rotatory power of starch
5 minutes	9.70 grams	182.1°
15	"	180.2
30	"	168
1 hour	"	168
1-1/2	"	164.6
2 hours	10.19	145.8
2-1/2	"	131.8
3	"	128.2
3-1/2	"	131.8
4	10.19	131.8

"Every stage in the coagulation of malt extract by heat is attended with a distinct modification of its starch transforming power; and conversely, we have never been able to discover any modification in starch transforming power which is not attended with distinct coagulation. In addition to this, at 80-81°, the point at which the diastatic power of malt extract is destroyed, nearly the whole of the coagulable albumenoids have been precipitated. We are consequently led to conclude that the diastatic power is a function of the coagulable albumenoids themselves, and is not due as has been generally supposed, to the presence of a distinctive transforming agent."[*]

We have already seen that the principal change which rice undergoes in its conversion to koji is the alteration in the nature of the albumenoid matter which becomes more easily degraded and soluble in water; taking this in connection with the destruction of the active properties of the solution at a temperature corresponding to that at which the albumenoid matter becomes coagulated, we are led to the conclusion that there is a similar connection between the presence of soluble albumenoids and the activity of the solution of koji which seems to hold in the case of malt extract.

[*] Journ. Chem. Soc, 1876, vol. II., p. 125, also 1879. Trans. p.770.

[†] Ibid., 1879 Trans. p. 596.

[*] loc.cit., 1879, Trans, p. 630.

[*] Brown and Heron, loc.cit., p. 651.

PART II: SAKE BREWING

Chapter 6. Preparation of Moto

The process of preparing sake followed in the large breweries of Itami and Nishinomiya is very nearly the same, and may be easily divided into distinct periods, but sake is also very frequently prepared in much smaller establishments, in which case, properly speaking, only two divisions can be noticed, viz. the preparation of *moto*, and the principal process. The chemical changes which occur will be very easily understood after the details which have been given in the preceding part, but it will not be found possible to make a distinct separation between the solution of the starch and the actual fermentation as can be done in beer brewing. In that industry the starch is converted into sugar and dextrin during the operation of mashing, after which the diastase is destroyed by boiling before the fermentation is allowed to begin, but in the manufacture of sake these two processes go on at the same time, except during the first few days. In this respect, therefore, the brewing of sake differs from that of beer, and it may, perhaps, be one of the reasons why the former liquid is so much more alcoholic than the latter.

As carried out at Itami and Nishinomiya sake brewing consists of the following series of processes:

1. Preparation of *moto*
2. Preparation of *soye*
3. Preparation of *naka*
4. Preparation of *shimai*
5. Filtration and clarification

Of these that which requires most care and is most liable to fail is the first, the preparation of moto.

MOTO

In the preparation of moto steamed rice, koji, and water are used in proportions which differ slightly in different works. The term *moto* is used to express not only the product of this operation, but also a definite amount—thus the workmen speak of one moto, two and a half moto, and so on. At Itami, the most famous district, the proportions for moto are:

Steamed rice   0.5 koku

Koji   0.2 koku

Water   0.6 koku
                    —————
                    1.3 koku

It may be remarked that the numbers indicating the mount of steamed rice and koji used refer, not to the finished products, but to the quantity of rice taken to form them.

At Nishinomiya, another very celebrated sake making district, the proportions are as follow:

Steamed rice   0.5 koku

Koji   0.2 koku

Water   0.63 koku
                    —————
                    1.33 koku

At a brewery in Tokyo at which I had the opportunity of watching the whole process from beginning to end and of making analyses of the mash at different periods, the proportions for one moto were:

Steamed rice   0.4 koku

Koji   0.16 koku

Water   0.4 koku
                    —————
                    0.96 koku

To find the percentages of dry rice and water in the last mixture we proceed as follows. The weight of one koku of water is 48 kuwamme (B.S. Lyman, Geological Survey. Report. Progress. 1878-79) and we have already seen that the weight of one koku of rice is on the average 40 kuwamme, hence the weight of one moto is:

Rice (for steaming)	16 kw.
Rice (for making koji)	6.4 kw.
Water	19.2 kw.

After steaming, the rice used was found to contain 38.8% water, hence the original rice, which contained 14% water had taken up in addition 40% of its weight in water. 16 kuwamme of rice will thus take up 6.4 kw. of water, which, together with the 14% already present, will give 6.4 + 2.24 = 8.64 kw. of water and 13.76 kw. of dry rice.

By the conversion of rice into koji 100 parts of common rice form 108 parts of koji containing 30% water, thus 6.4 kw. of rice will form 6.9 kw. of koji, containing 4.83 kw. dry rice and 2.07 kw. of water.

The total dry rice, therefore, is 13.76 + 4.83 = 18.59 kw. The water taken up is 8.64 + 2.07 = 10.71

The water subsequently added is 19.2, added to the 10.71 gives 29.91 kw., or in percentages:

Dry rice	38.3% (32.17 of starch)
Water	61.7%
	100.0%

The quantity taken for 1 moto is mixed and divided into six equal parts, each of which is placed in a shallow wooden tub called *hangiri*, of a capacity of 0.267 koku. The mass is thoroughly mixed by hand for two hours, any lumps which are formed being broken down. At first the mixture of rice, koji, and water is so thick that it would hardly fall out if the vessels were inverted, but in a short time it loses its stiffness and becomes thin. After 24 hours have elapsed stirring with paddles (*kai*) begins, and when this is finished the whole is thrown into a larger tub (*moto-oroshi*), provided with a cover cut in two to facilitate the inspection of its contents, and covered with matting for the purpose of diminishing loss of heat as much as possible. The preceding operations have been carried on at a low temperature, from 0°C to 9 or 10°C at the highest, and the chemical change which occurs during this period will be easily understood from the account already given of the action of koji upon gelatinized starch. The rice grains having been steamed are of course in the gelatinized state, but, owing to the greater compactness of the grain, the action is much less rapid than in the experiment carried out at 4 to 10°C as described earlier. Doubtless the mixture at first contains a certain proportion of maltose, as well as dextrose and dextrin, but it will be gradually changed into dextrose. The duration of this simple digestion in the cold differs in the different works and even in the same place. At Nishinomiya, an interval of one day after transference into one vessel is allowed before the mixture is warmed; at Itami it is sometimes heated at once, and sometimes kept for five or six days. At the Tokyo brewery, the mash was heated at 3 p.m. on the fifth day after mixing, and the two following analyses show its composition before that event took place.

	Third day, 8 a.m.	Fifth day, 8 a.m.
Dextrose	7.35	12.25
Dextrin	5.12	5.69
Glycerin, ash, albumenoids, etc.	trace	0.48
Fixed acid	0.017	0.019
Volatile acid	–	0.008
Water (by difference)	87.513	81.553
	100.0	100.0
Specific rotatory power	124°	106°
Specific gravity of mash	1.15	1.18
Temperature of mash	13°C.	10°C
Starch undissolved	20.43%	15.46%

The effect thus far has been to increase the amount of dextrose at the expense of the starch; at the same time a fresh proportion of dextrin is no doubt formed, but this increase is obscured by the fact that there are two actions going on, formation of dextrin by a splitting up of the starch, and a disappearance of dextrin by the hydrating action of the koji, and the result of these two actions is to leave the dextrin very nearly what it was on the third day. It is important to observe that even so early as the third day only dextrose, and no maltose, is present in solution; the observed specific rotatory power is 124°, and that calculated for dextrose and dextrin in the observed proportions is 123.4°. The specific gravity of the mash has increased a little owing to the larger amount of solid matter in the solution, and the specific rotatory power has diminished, the proportion of dextrose to dextrin being greater on the fifth day than on the third day. The composition of the mash as given on the fifth day may probably be looked upon as the usual composition just before heating; this sample was taken at 8 a.m. and the heating commenced at 3 p.m. on the same day. If no change had occurred the mash would have contained 32.17% starch. The dextrose and dextrin on the third day correspond to 11.735, which leaves 20.43% of starch undissolved, and in the same way the starch undissolved on the fifth day amounts to 15.46%.

The heating is effected in all establishments in the same way. A closed tub called *kumume* or *daki* of a somewhat conical form, 18 inches high, 12 inches at its upper diameter and 9 to 10 inches in diameter at the lower part, is filled with boiling water and tightly closed. It is supported by means of a handle formed by a cross bar fastened to two ears which project upwards from opposite sides; in this way it is let down into the thick mash contained in the large tub, and the mixture is agitated by moving the heater about. As a rule one heater is allowed to remain in the mash for a half a day, and is then replaced by a fresh one which is left in for the same time, but the number of heaters used depends to some extent upon the temperature of the air. During the 13 days required for the completion of the moto at Itami from 5 to 9 heaters are employed, and at Nishinomiya from 10 to 13 are used in the same time. It is found undesirable to raise the temperature of the mash too rapidly, probably because a too high temperature at first would allow the acid ferments to become developed to the exclusion of the alcoholic ferments.

In the Tokyo brewery the heaters were allowed to remain in the mash for a much shorter time. Introduced on the fifth day at 3 p.m. the liquid was transferred back from the large tub into the shallow pans on the eighth day at 7 a.m. and was allowed to cool as much as possible until the fourteenth day at 11 a.m. when a fresh addition of rice and koji was made, the commencement of the main process.

The heating of the mash has the effect of inducing alcoholic fermentation to set in with great vigor. On the seventh day, when the next sample was taken, gas was rising rapidly through the mash and on coming to the surface burst with a slight, explosive noise. At the same time a very strong, sharp odor was perceptible, whilst a foam covered the surface. The following analyses (Table 23) give the composition of the moto from the seventh to the fourteenth day, after which the main process began. The mash was again placed in the shallow *hangiri* at 7 a.m. on the 8th day.

Table 23: Composition of moto from 7th to 14th day

	Day 7	Day 10	Day 12	Day 14
Alcohol	5.2 %	8.61%	9.41%	9.20%
Dextrose	5.4	0.99	0.49	0.50
Dextrin	7.0	2.81	2.72	2.57
Glycerin, ash, albumenoid, etc.	1.14	2.82	2.35	1.93
Fixed acid	0.31	0.24	0.31	0.30
Volatile acid	0.15	0.11	0.05	0.03
Water (by difference)	80.80	84.42	84.67	85.47
	100%	100%	100%	100%
Specific rotatory power	135°	100.7°	111.6°	116°
Specific gravity of the mash	1.08	1.05	1.06	1.04
Temperature of the mash	23°C	14°C	10°C	9°C
Starch undissolved	10.68%	12.46%	11.55%	12.05%

The alcoholic fermentation set in somewhat rapidly, for between 3 p.m. on the fifth day and 8 a.m. on the seventh day 5% of alcohol was formed, and the dextrose diminished from 12.25% to 5.4%. The amount of dextrin increased in that time, but the increase is probably only apparent, caused by the loss of matter in the form of carbonic acid. The solution of starch during this stage does not appear to have gone on very actively; there is a discrepancy in the numbers calculated on the seventh to the fourteenth days, which probably arises from the difficulty of taking an average sample of the mash. The percentages given are calculated on the original weight of the mash.

From the seventh to the fourteenth day the alcohol steadily increases; the dextrose is very quickly removed, there being less than 1% on the tenth day, and between the seventh and the tenth the dextrin is reduced from 7% to 2.8% about which it remains during the rest of the time, owing probably to the koji having lost its activity.

When the liquid was heated by the introduction of hot water barrels the temperature attained was 23° in the Tokyo brewery, and 25°C at Nishinomiya. As soon as the mash was transferred to the shallow tubs, however, it began to cool down, the activity of the fermentation not being sufficient to keep up the temperature; the composition of the liquid indeed, shows that this result must follow inasmuch as there is not enough food left in the liquid in the form of sugar and dextrin to allow the active growth of the ferment to continue. Hence on the tenth day the temperature fell to 14°C, on the twelfth day to 10°C and on the fourteenth day to 9°C.

A sample of the finished moto obtained from the brewery at Nishinomiya had the following composition, which agrees very well with that obtained in Tokyo, from which it may be inferred that different specimens of moto will not differ in composition to any marked extent.

Finished Moto from Nishinomiya

Alcohol	10.5%
Dextrose	0.2%
Total acid	0.56%
Starch and cellulose	16.58%
Water (by difference)	72.16%
	100%

The chemical changes which go on in the production of moto are sufficiently easily explained in general terms. During the first days, whilst the mixture is kept at a low temperature, the koji is acted upon by the water and the solution then attacks the starch according to the reactions already indicated. This results in the production of a saccharine and dextrinous liquid forming a suitable food for the ferment which subsequently establishes itself in the liquid on warming. How the ferment appears will be discussed in a later section. Whilst the yeast is growing and converting the sugar into alcohol, the solution of starch and the hydration of dextrin by the koji still continue so long as the latter retains its activity, but that appears to be destroyed some time before the moto is completely finished. At the end of this stage the yeast ferment though not vigorous, is well formed and only requires a fresh addition of food to commence growing with renewed activity. It may, indeed, be said that the preparation of moto has for its main object the production of a healthy ferment, so that the use of the moto in the subsequent operations answers very nearly to the yeast added to the wort in beer brewing.

The sake brewer judges of the progress of the moto by the vigor of the fermentation and by the taste of the liquid. At Itami it is said to require 13 days to obtain the proper taste; after three days the taste is sweet owing to the presence of much dextrose; after six days it is astringent, on the seventh day is slightly alcoholic, and finally, it becomes sour. When finished the brewer is able to distinguish five tastes, respectively sweet, sour, bitter, astringent, and alcoholic, and of these the sour, bitter, and astringent are most pronounced. The formation of the acid is also formed during the time the mash is allowed to cool in the shallow vessels, although its amount cannot be very large seeing the great development which the yeast has taken. The bitter and astringent tastes are due to the presence of the yeast, though the nature of the substances giving rise to them is unknown.

Chapter 7. The Principal Process

In the chief fermentation process as carried out at Itami and Nishinomiya there are three stages, called respectively *soye*, *naka*, and *shimai*, although they do not differ from one another in any essential particular. In the Tokyo brewery it is not so easy to distinguish these stages, and it will, therefore, be most convenient to describe the former methods first, reserving the latter and the analyses of the product at different times until the others have been disposed of.

At Itami the proportions used to one moto are the following:

Moto	1.30 koku
Steamed rice	1.30 koku
Koji	0.35 koku
Water	1.30 koku
	4.25 koku

At Nishinomiya the following quantities are used:

Moto	1.33 koku
Steamed rice	1.05 koku
Koji	0.35 koku
Water	1.15 koku
	3.88 koku

This mixture is placed in a large tun called *sanjaku-oke* (or three-foot tub) which holds about 8 koku, and which is therefore, only about half filled. The mixture is stirred every two hours, and, after 42 hours at Itami and 3 days Nishinomiya, the first stage (soye) is finished, and the product is divided into two parts preparatory to the second stage. During this period fermentation sets in and the temperature rises, that of one batch examined at Itami being 20°C the temperature of the air at the same time being 11°C. An odor, strong, pungent, and fragrant arose from the mash. A sample of the mash from Nishinomiya had the following composition.

Alcohol	11.0%
Dextrose	0.18%
Total acid	0.36%
Starch	17.52%
	29.06%

The amount of dextrose present is very small, a fact which is probably accounted for by the continuous growth of the ferment between the time when the sample was taken and the time of its analysis. The alcohol on that account is doubtless higher than in the mash at the end of this stage.

As soon as the first stage is finished the mash is divided into two parts each of which is placed in a three-foot tub, and a fresh amount of steamed rice, koji, and water added in the following proportions, using the whole of the soye.

At Itami they use:

Soye	4.25 koku
Steamed rice	2.00 koku
Koji	0.65 koku
Water	3.00 koku
	9.90 koku

At Nishinomiya, the following mixture is made:

Soye	3.88 koku
Steamed rice	1.80 koku
Koji	0.60 koku
Water	2.40 koku
	8.68 koku

The stirring is continued every two hours as in the soye stage so that the grains of rice may not fall to the bottom, and get beyond the action of koji. The mixture is left for 24 hours by which time the *naka* stage is finished. At Itami the temperature observed was lower than in the soye stage, but the observation was made soon after mixing so that the fermentation had not then had time to fully develop itself; the temperature observed was 15°C that of the air being 11°C. This mash also possessed a pungent, fragrant odor though not so powerful as in the case of the soye.

After the lapse of 24 hours, that is at the end of the second (naka) stage, the quantity of material in each tub is again divided into two, so that each of these parts now contains only one-fourth of the original moto. To the whole a fresh admixture of steamed rice, koji, and water is made—at Itami in the following proportions:

Naka	9.90 koku
Steamed rice	3.30 koku
Koji	1.00 koku
Water	4.20 koku
	18.40 koku

At Nishinomiya, the following proportions are used:

Naka	8.68 koku
Steamed rice	3.60 koku
Koji	1.20 koku
Water	6.20 koku
	19.68 koku

The quantity of water added at this stage (shimai) depends on the alcoholic strength required. At first the whole quantity is divided amongst four tubs, but after standing for about 3 days the mixture is collected by degrees into one large tub called *roku-shaku-oke*, holding about 24 or 25 koku. In this the fermentation goes on more vigorously for two or three days after which it gradually ceases—the froth sinks, and the liquid is now strongly alcoholic and ready for filtration. The time during which it is allowed to stand before filtration varies, but is not a matter of much importance.

It may be useful to collect together the amounts of each material used:

Table 24: Itami

Stages	Rice for steaming	Rice for koji	Water
Moto	0.5 koku	0.2 koku	0.6 koku
Soye	1.3 koku	0.35 koku	1.8 koku
Naka	2.0 koku	0.65 koku	3.0 koku
Shimai	8.3 koku	1.0 koku	4.2 koku
	7.1 koku	2.2 koku	9.1 koku
	284 kuwamme	88 kuwamme	436.8 kuwamme

284 kuwamme of rice contain 244.24 kuwamme of dry rice and 39.76 kw. of water. It also takes up in addition, by steaming, 113.6 kw. of water—hence the total weight of water is 153.36 kw.

88 kuwamme of rice after being converted into koji weigh 95.04 kw. and the koji contains 66.53 kw. of dry rice and 28.51 kw. of water.

We have, therefore:

	Dry rice	Water
Steamed rice	244.24 kw.	153.36 kw.
Koji	66.53 kw.	28.51 kw.
Water	-0-	436.kw
	310.77 kw.	618.67 kw.

or in percentages:

Dry rice	32.3 % (containing 27.13 starch)
Water	67.7 %
	100%

We may now consider the method of brewing followed in Tokyo. One feature is that the frequent subdivision of the mash does not take place as in Itami and Nishinomiya, but after the moto has been finished, it is transferred to a large tub (*rokushaku oke*) and the subsequent additions are made to it in the same vessel. This must result in a saving both of material and of labor, and at the same time the temperature required for the active growth of the ferment is better maintained as will be seen from the observations which will be recorded presently.

In the description of the preparation of moto the last analysis given of the mash was at 8 a.m. on the fourteenth day. The next sample was taken at 8 a.m. on the seventeenth day, when the main process was already entered upon. To the quantity of material one moto the following amounts of rice and koji were added at 11 a.m. on the fourteenth day.

Steamed rice	1.0 koku
Koji	0.3 koku
Water	1.2 koku
Moto	0.96 koku
	3.46 koku

A second addition was made at 11 a.m. on the sixteenth day, amounting to:

Steamed rice	1.2 koku
Koji	0.36 koku
Water	1.44 koku
Already mixed	3.46 koku
	6.46 koku

Supposing that no alteration had taken place in the mixture, the quantities of dry rice and water present in the mash, including the first addition, would be:

Dry rice	34.9 % (containing 29.32 starch)
Water	65.1 %
	100%

A sample of the mash taken on the seventeenth day from the commencement had the following composition:

Alcohol	5.8 %
Dextrose	2.06 %
Dextrin	3.890 %
Glycerin, albumenoids etc.	0.043 %
Fixed acid	0.015%
Water	88.192%
	100 %

Undissolved starch & cellulose	12.814 %
Specific rotatory power	160°
Specific gravity of mash	1.03
Temperature of mash	19°C

The specific rotatory power of the solution is as high as 160° because the percentage of dextrin in the solid matter is so large, amounting to 65% of the total solid matter in solution. The number calculated for the following is 160.7°.

Dextrin	65.00
Dextrose	34.36
Inactive matter	0.64
	100 %

Hence, at this stage also no maltose is present in solution, that first formed having been converted into dextrose.

The two additions of steamed rice, koji, and water on the fourteenth and sixteenth days, respectively, may perhaps be regarded as indicating the division of the main process into the stages *soye* and *naka*. If this be so the third addition which is made on the eighteenth day at noon will correspond with the commencement of the stage called *shimai* at Itami and Nishinomiya. The last addition consisted of:

Rice	1.40 koku
Koji	0.42 koku
Water	1.68 koku
Already present	6.46 koku
	9.96 koku

The weights and percentages of dry rice and water present, if no change had taken place, would be:

	Weight	Percentage
Dry rice	175.1 kw.	34.7% (29.15% starch)
Water	329.03 kw.	65.3 %
	504.13 kw.	100 %

The temperature of the mash at this stage rises considerably owing to the very active growth of the alcoholic ferment; thus on the seventeenth day the temperature rose to 19°C, on the nineteenth day to 25°C, and on the twenty-first day to 26°C, by which time the fermentation was for the most part finished, and the temperature then fell to 20°C on the twenty-fourth day and to 12°C on the twenty-eighth day. During this time the temperature of the air was never above 12°C and, for most of the time, far below that point. The composition of the mash during this the last stage of the main process will be seen from the accompanying analyses.

	Day 19	Day 21	Day 24	Day 28
Alcohol	9.44%	11.83%	12.41%	13.28%
Dextrose	1.16	0.27	0.27	-0-
Dextrin	2.74	1.42	0.47	0.41
Glycerin, albumenoids, etc.	1.09	1.98	1.68	1.99
Fixed acid	0.08	0.058	0.086	0.107
Volatile acid		0.029	0.086	0.061
Water	85.54	84.413	84.998	84.202
	100	100	100	100
Specific rotatory power	132.8°	88.8°	48.2°	36°
Specific gravity of mash	1.017	0.994	0.990	0.988
Temperature of mash	25°C	26°C	20°C	12°C
Undissolved starch	7.85%	5.534%	5.40%	4.18%

A glance at the numbers given in this table will show how far the fermentation has been carried. After the addition made on the eighteenth day, the mash was left to itself except for the stirring which was continued as before about every two hours. During this time a vigorous growth of ferment went on, gas escaped rapidly, and a pungent odor was spread throughout the chamber. On the nineteenth day the effervescence was very strong, and it rose to a maximum between that day and the twenty-first day when, although the temperature was higher, the amount of effervescence was perceptibly less. The taste of the mash was bitter and strongly alcoholic. On the twenty-fourth day the effervescence was very slight and the odor was strongly ethereal, but although the effervescence had diminished greatly, formation of alcohol still went on, as between the twenty-fourth and twentyeighth days the percentage increased from 12.41% to 13.23%. How much further the process might have been carried is doubtful; at this time the undissolved matter was separated from the alcoholic solution and analyses could not be continued, but from the analysis of the mixture on the twenty-eighth day compared with that on the twenty-fourth day it appears that the diastase of the koji was not yet destroyed. The amount of dextrose and dextrin which disappeared during that interval was not sufficient to account for the increase in the amount of alcohol, which must therefore, have been formed by the solution of a fresh quantity of starch.

From the numbers giving the percentage of undissolved starch it will be seen that it suffers a constant diminution, a change which shows that the solution of the starch under the influence of the koji is a continuous process, going on concurrently with the fermentation of the sugar formed. Indeed, it would appear that the conversion of the sugar into alcohol is a more rapid process than the production of sugar from starch, if it were otherwise, we might expect the sugar to increase at first, or at any rate, to remain more nearly constant than it does.

A point of interest is the increase in the amount of fixed acid from the nineteenth day onwards. The numbers given are calculated for sulfuric acid, although the acid present is for the most part succinic acid, but even in the last analysis its amount is much less than was found during the preparation of moto. In that stage, however, owing to the greater surface exposed to the air, and the lower activity of the alcoholic fermentation, other organisms are present, lactic acid ferments especially, and these contribute to the larger amount of fixed acid in the moto.

Chapter 8. Fermentation of the Mash

In the previous sections we have seen that the sugar formed by the action of the koji upon the starch of the rice grain undergoes fermentation, that is, is converted into alcohol, carbonic acid, and some other products in smaller quantity. It is now generally admitted that the production of these bodies is the result of the growth of some form of organism, which, in the majority of cases, is a species of the genus Saccharomyces. In beer brewing the yeast ferment is added to the wort after cooling, and then finding the necessary food present it goes on growing and budding rapidly, producing, in addition to the substance of the newly formed cells, alcohol and carbonic acid as the results of its growth. These cells when examined under the microscope have the appearance (shown in Figure 9) of small spherical or oval cells, having a longer diameter of about one-hundredth of a millimeter and frequently with small bubbles in the interior. They grow by a process of budding, that is, a small protuberance forms at the side of a full grown cell, it breaks away, and then acts on its own account. In the fermentation of beer the most important species of alcoholic ferment is the one just alluded to, Saccharomyces cerevisaie.

In the manufacture of wine no ferment is directly added to the must, but it has been found that germs of the alcoholic ferments which subsequently grow and produce the wine adhere to the outside of the skin and stalks of the grape and in that way enter the liquid when the grapes are crushed. The common ferment of wine is Saccharomyces ellipsoideus, but other species are also found, such as S. pastorianus, S. exiguus, S. Conglomeratus, and Carpozyma apiculatum. The following are the average dimensions of these species:

	Long Diameter	Short diameter
Saccharomyces ellipsoideus	0.006 mm	0.004–0.005 mm
S. Pastorianus	0.006	variable
S. exiguus	0.003	0.0025
S. conglomeratus	0.006	
S. mycoderma	0.006	0.004
Carpozyma apiculatum	0.006	0.003

Figure 9: Cells of saccharomyces cerivisae. Skurada beer brewery. Tokyo. x 100.

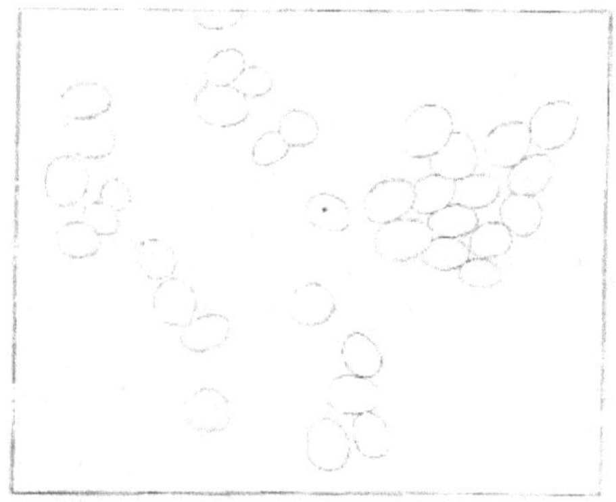

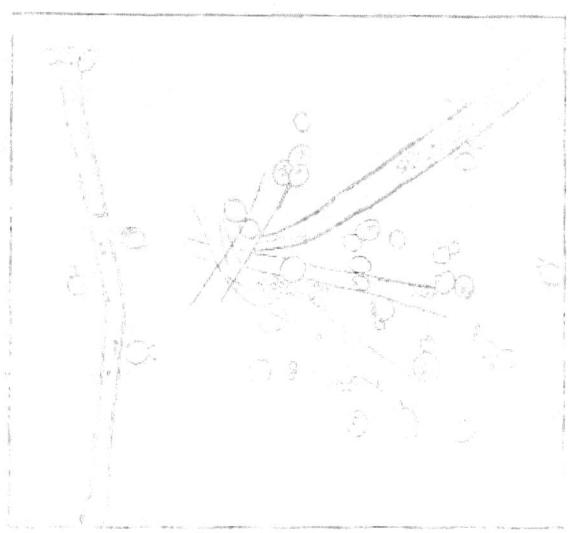

The ferment of beer, therefore, is much larger than any of these species, and although the full grown specimens vary a little in size, they never fall below 0.008 mm in diameter.M. Pasteur has, however, shown that under certain conditions S. Pastorianus may assume very different forms and sizes.

Besides these special alcoholic ferments there are other forms of fungi which are capable of yielding alcohol when they are caused to grown submerged in a saccharine solution. Such are especially the Mucor mucedo and the Mucor racemosus which have been examined by Fitz. They however, never yield a liquid containing more than from 2 to 4 percent alcohol.

Before considering the nature and origin of the ferment which is found in sake breweries, it will be convenient to describe the microscopic appearances presented by the mash at the periods at which the chemical analyses described in the last section were made.

On the first and second days after mixing no appearances of any special interest were to be observed, but on the third day, together with fragments of broken mycelium filled with granulations, isolated cells of ferment were to be seen as represented in Figure 11; the largest of these were only 0.0075 millimeter in diameter. The temperature of the mash at that time 13°C, but it contained no appreciable amount of alcohol. The existence of these cells, however, at this very early stage is of considerable interest, and that they were capable of developing rapidly when placed under the proper conditions is shown by the appearance of a sample which was placed near a stove and left till the following day; represented in Figure 12. In this case large numbers of ferment cells are to be seen, of two kinds, one nearly spherical the largest measuring 0.0081 mm in diameter, and the other longer and almost cylindrical. The appearance was that of an actively growing yeast.

Figure 11: Mash of third day x 740.

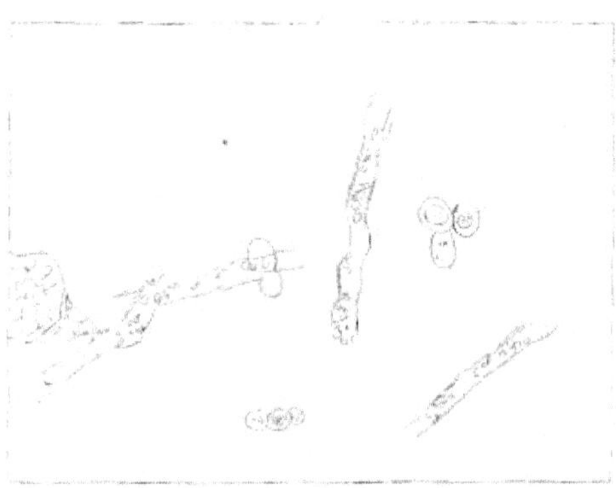

Figure 12: Mash of third day after standing 3 days. x 740.

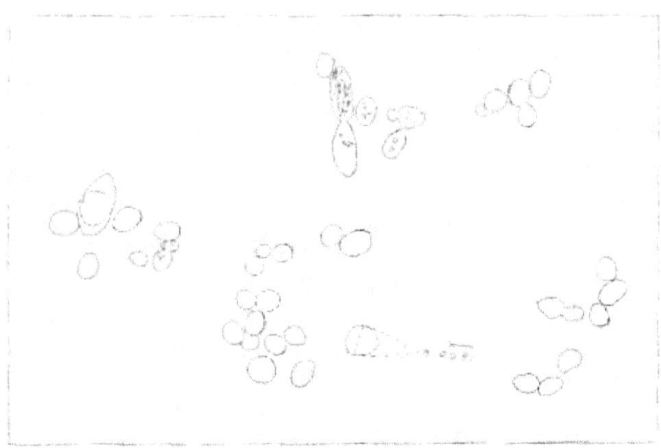

The mash which was left under the usual conditions did not alter thus in appearance. A few more cells may be observed associated with fragments of mycelium, and with others apparently bursting and scattering a fine dust, but there was no active growth, nor did analysis indicate the formation of any alcohol. The appearance of the mash on the fifth day is shown in Figure 13.

Figure 13: Mash of the fifth day, x740.

After the last sample was taken the moto was heated, and almost immediately a great development of the ferment cells took place. On the seventh day the temperature was 23°C and the microscopic appearance (Figure 14) shows that the cells were budding and growing with considerable activity, and chemical analysis at the same time indicated the existence of 5.2% alcohol. The diameter of the largest cell was 0.0083 millimeter and the average size 0.0076 mm. The mash on the tenth day had a very similar appearance to that on the seventh, and on the twelfth, although the temperature was then only 10°C, the cells still appeared fresh and vigorous as in the left of Figure 16. At the same time fragments of the mycelium were to be seen as well as a number of very minute cells, the functions of which are not known. On the fourteenth day the cells had much the same character as before, the largest still measuring about the same, i.e., 0.0082 mm.

The next sample examined was that taken on the seventeenth day, after the further addition of rice and koji, and when the temperature had risen to 19°C, sufficiently high to promote the very active growth of the yeast. Figure 17 shows the appearance of the ferment on that day, and it will be noticed that the size of the cells is rather less, the largest being only 0.0075 mm, perhaps because they were not fully grown. By the nineteenth day they were again in active growth, and the largest again had a long diameter of 0.0082 mm.

The temperature at that time was 25°C and the amount of alcohol increased from 5.8% on the seventeenth day to 9.44% on the nineteenth. The growth of the yeast continued, the temperature of the mash on the twenty-first day being 26°C, but there are to be observed in the figure of this mash other ferment cells, small straight or curved filaments which are the cause of the future deterioration of the sake. They resemble very closely the filaments which are found in "turned" beer and wine, and are also to be found in enormous numbers in sake which has become spoilt. (See Figure 25 and Figure 26).

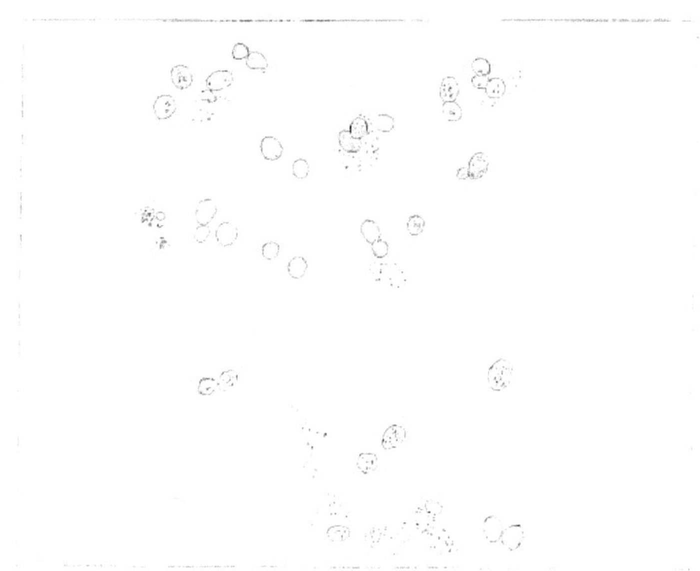

Figure 14: Mash of seventh day, x 720.

Figure 15: Mash of tenth day, x 730.

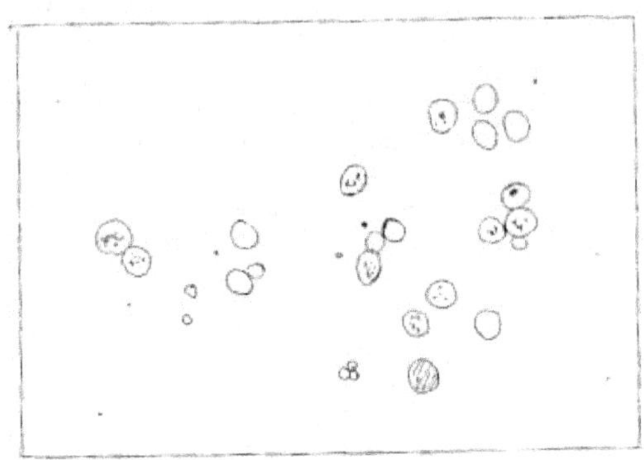

Figure 16: Mash of twelfth day, x 700.

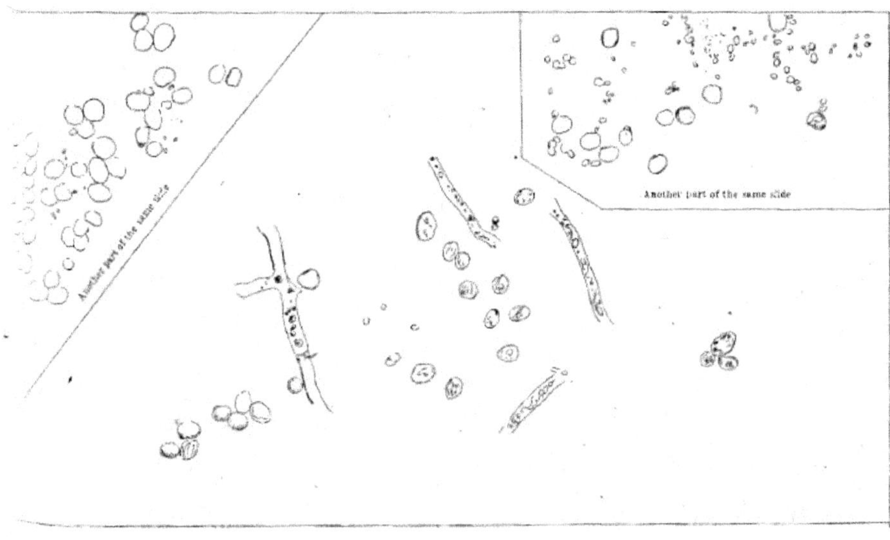

Figure 17: Mash of fourteenth day, x730.

Figure 18: Mash of seventeenth day, x 730.

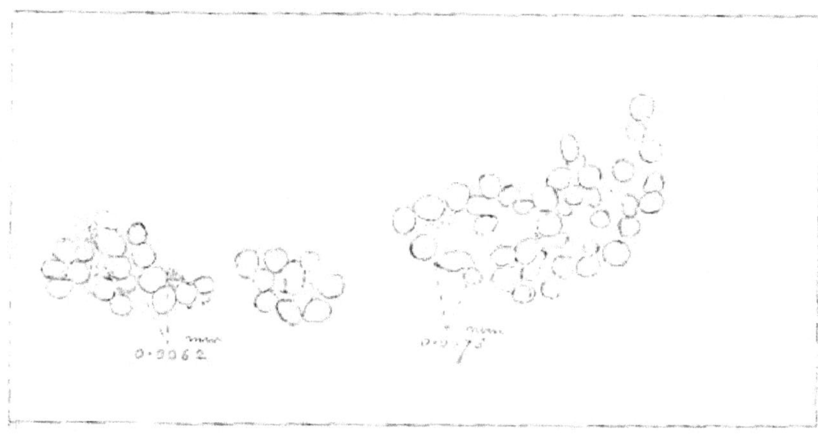

I have drawn also a filament of mycelium to show that it was still present, although as the ferment cells were very numerous and collected at the surface of the mash, the filaments appeared to be not so numerous as at first. The same remark applies to Figure 21 which represents the appearance of the mash on the twenty-fourth day, the last sample of the series which was examined. By this time the temperature had fallen to 20°C, but the fermentation still went on as the increase in the percentage of alcohol proved.

Figure 19: Mash of nineteenth day, x730.

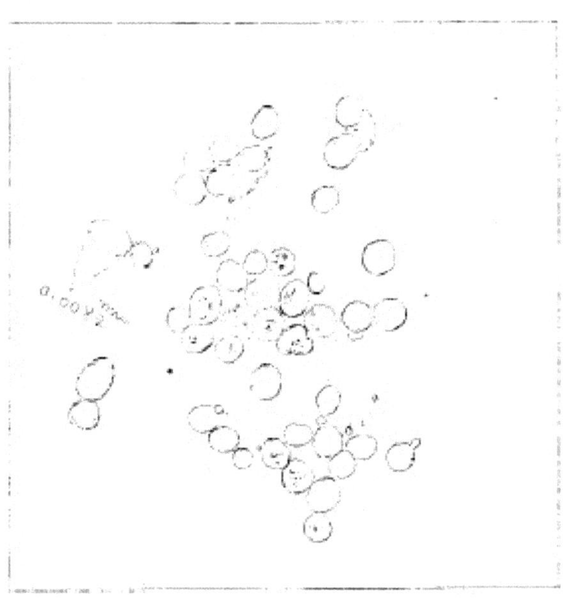

Figure 20: Mash of twenty-first day, x 730.

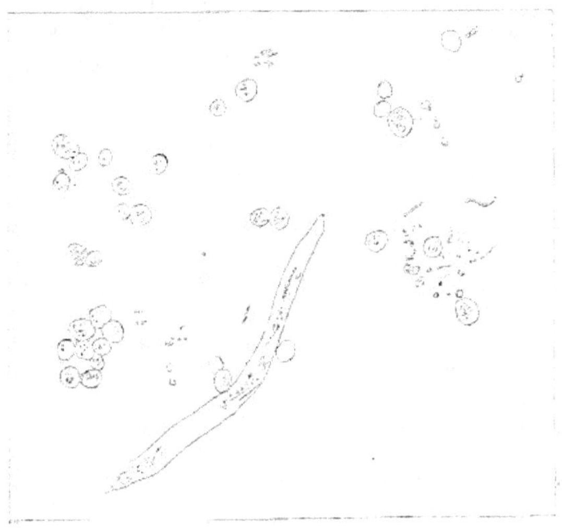

Figure 21: Mash of twenty-fourth day, x730.

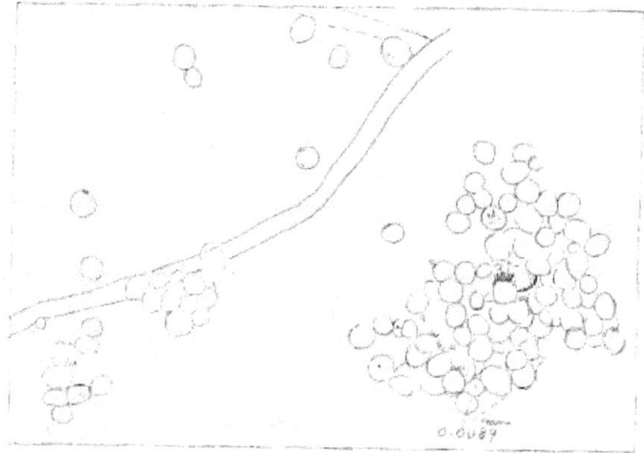

We have here a process of fermentation which resembles the wine fermentation in the fact that no ferment has been knowingly added by the brewer, and which belongs to the class called "spontaneous fermentations." By that term of course it is not meant that the living organisms have been generated spontaneously, without any forefathers, but only that they have appeared without intentional sowing. As the theory that living organisms are produced without the intervention of previous life has no basis of reality we are driven to enquire from what source these small particles of ferment have been derived. This has been discussed by Mr. Korschelt[*] in a paper read before the German Asiatic Society, and he very rightly says that we may conceive of their introduction in three different ways. In the first place he says that the grains of koji may carry upon their surface germs of the yeast in the same way that the grapes carry into the fermentation vat the cells which afterwards effect the conversion of sugar into alcohol. Or the germs of the yeast may in the second place fall into the vats from the atmosphere. To both explanations he considers that the sudden commencement of the fermentation is sufficient objection, for, as will be remembered, between the time of heating of the vat, and the time of taking the first sample afterwards, a period of 41 hours, more than 5% of alcohol had been formed. Mr. Korschelt, therefore, inclines to the third possibility, viz., that the mycelium fibers of the koji fungus have been changed into the ferment cells, and he bases this supposition upon the observations made by Du Bary and Rees that the mycelium of the two species of Mucor, M. mucedo and M. racemosus, have the property under certain conditions of forming cells which are able to convert sugar into alcohol.

The question is one of very great scientific interest, and no apology is therefore required for entering into a somewhat minute investigation of it. For a long time it was supposed that such common air fungi as Penicillium glaucum, and Spergillus glaucus might, under suitable conditions, be transformed in the ordinary alcoholic ferment, and in that state go on converting sugar into alcohol. M. Pasteur[‡] has put this theory to most rigorous tests, and has proved in the most conclusive manner the absence of any evidence whatever of such a transformation. He has shown that if proper care be taken to exclude every germ but the one being experimented upon, no conversion of that spore into any other species takes place. Thus a spore of Penicillium or of Aspergillus, or of Mycoderma vini will grow in ordinary wort so long as it has sufficient air to breathe and is provided with sufficient food, but it is never converted into what is usually termed an alcoholic ferment. At the same time if the air be excluded he finds that the plant will go on growing for a longer or shorter time after the exclusion of the oxygen, but that its life is then carried on under abnormal conditions, which is evidenced by a change in the form of the mycelial fibers, and by the fact that a certain amount of alcohol is produced. The mycelium becomes swollen and contorted, and shows a tendency to break up into small cells attached end to end, and it is only in this state that the plant is capable of forming alcohol, but it does this without the presence of a single cell of the common yeast. If the swollen mycelium cells be again allowed to grow under the usual conditions, that is with plenty of food and air, they reproduce the normal form of the plant from which the spores were originally taken. It may in fact be taken that while the fungus is healthy, growing under normal conditions, it consumes sugar, converting it into water and carbonic acid without producing any alcohol whatever, but that as soon as it no longer meets with the requisite quantity of free oxygen, still remaining in presence of sugar, it falls ill, and in that diseased condition it lives for a longer or a shorter time, producing alcohol as a pathological product. All fungi are not so easily killed, some may produce a very large quantity of alcohol before they die, and may even go on reproducing fresh cells. The Mucor mucedo, for instance, according to Fitz is killed when the liquid contains more than 1% alcohol, while the Mucor racemosus is more tenacious of life, and is not killed until the liquid contains from 2 to 4-1/2 %, according to different observers.* There may be all variations in the case of different fungi, and although no case is at present known of one of the common air fungi yielding a greater percentage of alcohol than that given by the Mucor racemosus, there is no inherent improbability in the supposition that some fungi may yield much more. In fact the chemical difference between what are usually termed ferments and the ordinary fungi, seems to be their power of living out of contact with free oxygen, deriving that which they require from sugar, and thus causing it to split up into various other products in the manner shown by some such equations as the following:

$$1 \qquad C^{12}H_{12}O_6 = 2\ C_2H_6O + 2\ CO_2$$

$$\text{Dextrose} \qquad\qquad \text{Alcohol}$$

$$2 \qquad 4\ C^6H_{12}O_6 + 3\ H^2O = C^4H_6O_4 + 6\ C^3H_8O_3 + 2\ CO_2 + O \text{ (Monoyer)}$$

$$\text{Dextrose} \qquad\qquad \underset{\text{acid}}{\text{Succinic}} \qquad \text{Glycerin}$$

Mr. Korschelt's supposition that the mycelium of the koji fungus itself breaks up and goes on living as a ferment would be remarkable, therefore, only in the fact that the cells were able to live in a liquid containing as much as 15% alcohol, a very much higher percentage than the common beer yeast can exist in. But the question naturally arises whether the conditions under which the fermentation is carried on are such as would permit a fungus which ordinarily grows in air to live with such results immersed in a liquid. M. Pasteur has shown that in proportion as the fungus is provided with air it grows without producing alcohol, and, if the conditions are such that the plant can get plenty of free oxygen, no alcohol will be formed. Even the ordinary brewers yeast at the beginning of the fermentation process grows in a vigorous manner but without producing alcohol, because it is at that time living upon the free oxygen dissolved in the wort, but by that means it acquires a freshness which enables it to grow at a later period with great vigor at the expense of the sugar contained in the wort. M. Pasteur thus explains the custom of aerating the wort followed in distilleries and in works for the manufacture of yeast. Are not the same conditions to be found in the manufacture under discussion? During the first few days the mixture of rice, koji, and water, divided as it is amongst a number of small vessels, exposes a large surface which allows it to become perfectly saturated with air, so that, when the whole quantity of liquid is collected in one large tub and heated the ferment is enabled to grow vigorously, and as soon as the air has been used up, to produce alcohol at the expense of the sugar formed in the previous stage. We can readily understand that these conditions would be suitable for the growth of such a form of ferment as beer yeast, which shows very little tendency to assume the air form (aerobian), but they appear to be less suited to the growth of a mycelium, such as that of the Eurotium. In fact until the mass is collected into the single vat, if the mycelium grows at all, it will form long, thin filaments, which will not produce alcohol, and it will only be when all the oxygen has been exhausted that any alcohol will be produced. Before very long, however, the mash is allowed to cool down by being again spread out in shallow vessels, and during this time, as a large surface is exposed the air, the mash will again become charged with oxygen, and no more alcohol should be formed. What do we actually find? The heating in the large tub lasted in the brewing operation, described earlier, from 3 p.m. on the fifth day until 7 a.m. on the eight day, after which the mixture was transferred to the shallow vessels. Yet even after the tenth day the amount of alcohol increased, not much it is true, because the temperature conditions were unfavorable, but enough to show the fermentative activity of the yeast. If we had to do with an air-fungus, it would not be expected that the formation of alcohol would go on under such conditions, but it is quite what would be expected from the growth of a common yeast.

Again, during the main process, the mash is continually aerated by repeated beating, and we can hardly reconcile this with the production of the large amount of alcohol if the ferment were like the submerged mycelial fibers of a Penicilium or an Aspergillus. Such treatment, however, would be quite compatible with the active growth and fermentative activity of a species of saccharomyces, and would indeed answer to the aeration of the wort practiced by distillers.

Further, in the drawings illustrating the microscopic appearance of the ferment during the fermentation, portions of mycelium will be observed at all stages, and yet in no case was there observed any thickening such as M. Pasteur has figured in figures 20 and 21 (English edition) in the case of Aspergillus glaucus and Mucor racemosus, and in Plate VI. and figure 24 of Mucor mucedo.[*] The mycelium remained of the same form throughout the series of observations made at the brewery and only changed in appearance from the presence of minute granulations, probably some form of foreign organism which found a resting place within the fibers. Mr. Korschelt has referred to this appearance, as well as to the more frequent crossings in the mycelium, as one of the reasons for supposing that the ferment cells observed are actually different forms of the original mycelium. I have not been able to satisfy myself that the crossings of the mycelium are more frequent after the plant has been submerged for some time than at first, but even if it were so, it does not seem that it would necessarily have any bearing upon the question. Nor am I able to agree with Mr. Korschelt when he says that there is a marked difference in the abundance of the mycelium at the beginning and the end. The point upon which most stress is laid is the suddenness of the fermentation, and that it does appear suddenly is a matter about which no one can have any doubt; but is there not a very simple explanation of it apart from the transformation of the mycelium into ferment cells? The fermentation appears immediately after the warming of the mash, which has already been exposed to the air in shallow vessels for several days before being gathered into a single vessel. It is also allowed to remain in the tub for several hours before heating, during which time we may suppose that a large part of the dissolved oxygen has been absorbed by the ferment. By heating the temperature is raised to about 25°C and that we know is very favorable for the growth of yeast. Knowing how rapidly the yeast plant buds under the conditions, it does not appear to be necessary to invoke the transformation of the mycelium into ferment cells in order to account for the sudden appearance of the fermentation, and to my mind the simple and natural explanation is that the fermentation is spontaneous, that the germs are found either on the koji used, or attached to the vessels in which the operations are performed. Mr. Korschelt has referred to the fact that on one occasion, before the fermentation had properly developed itself, I observed some completely cylindrical cells. Unfortunately I did not take sketches of these cells at the time, but it is probably that they were some species of mycoderma, introduced accidentally. I have repeatedly digested koji with water without observing any change in the appearance of the mycelium. The successive changes usually seen are represented with sufficient clearness in Figure 22, Figure 23, and Figure 24. A quantity of koji was placed in a flask with some water, the flask corked and provided with a delivery tube leading into water, and then left near a stove. After two days a drop withdrawn and examined under the microscope appeared as shown in Figure 22, enlarged 730 diameters. Any one comparing this drawing with either figure 10 or figure 11 of

M. Pasteur's work "Sur la Biere", which represent alcoholic ferments directly derived from the atmosphere, will see the close resemblance they bear to one another, and will hardly entertain any doubt concerning their atmospheric origin. On allowing this flask to remain for two days longer, there was a slight difference observable, the number of cells of alcoholic ferment had increased, and after three days more fermentation was very active, and an apparently pure specimen of yeast was obtained. Comparing these three stages of fermentation, can any one doubt that the germs of the alcoholic ferment were originally present in the koji, and on being subjected to the proper conditions developed.

It is, of course, a matter of great difficulty to prove any proposition of this kind, but the probability appears to my mind to be very greatly in favor of the hypothesis that the germs have been either air sown or were adherent to the grains of koji before use.

The average size of the fully grown ferment cell is about 0.0082 millimeter, that is, between that of the ordinary wine ferment, and that of the beer yeast. From the many different appearances which the Saccharomyces Pastorianus puts on, it is difficult to say whether this ferment cell agrees in species with any of the European ferments, but from the large proportion of alcohol in the liquid in which it can exist, it appears to differ from beer yeast. The ferment of wine may produce a liquid containing as much as 15% alcohol, and from this resemblance as well as from the origin of the fermentation, sake making approaches more nearly the wine than the beer manufacture.

Figure 22: Koji in water left for two days, x730.

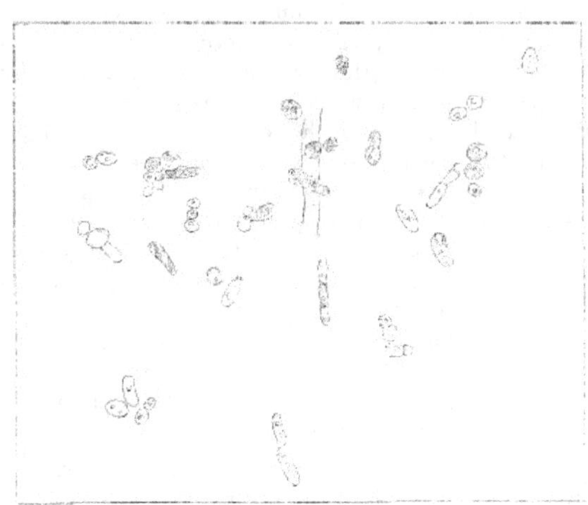

Figure 23: Same as last; left in warm place for two days longer, x730.

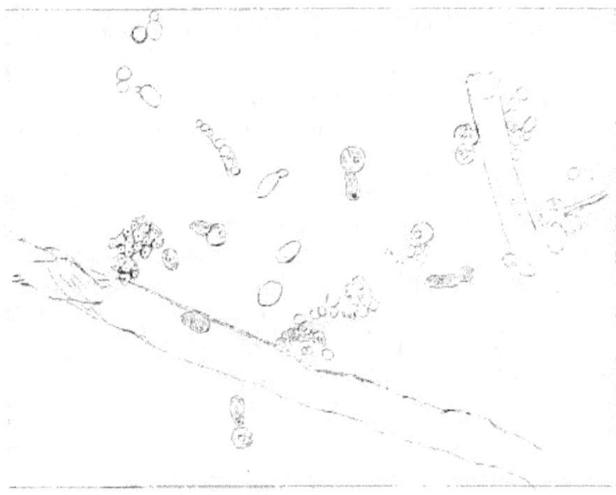

Figure 24: Same as last two, last left for three days more, x730.

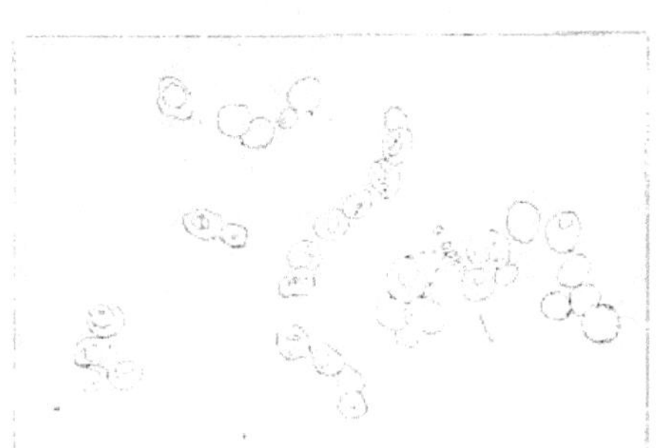

---

*. Mitt. der Deutsch. Gessells. 16tes Heft., p. 258.

†. Etudes sur la Biere, 1876, p. 86, English translation, p. 86 et seq.

*. 4-1/2 % (Brefeld), 3.3 to 3.4 % (Pasteur), 2.3 to 2.7% (Fitz).

*. I have grown the "tane" (spores) in boiled malt wort, and though the mycelium produced was kept submerged, no change in its form resulted, nor did cells of alcohol ferment make their appearance.

Chapter 9. Filtration of Sake and Yield of Alcohol

At the end of the fermentation the mash is very thin and consists mainly of alcohol and water with a small quantity of the unaltered rice grains suspended in the liquid. The subsequent processes are essentially the same everywhere and it will not be necessary to refer in detail to the methods followed in different breweries. The separation of the liquid from the suspended matter is effected by the use of wooden press called *fune*, a sketch of which is given in Figure 1 on page 3.

It consists of a wooden box covered on the top by a wooden plate of rather smaller size which is pressed down upon the mass beneath by means of a long lever weighted at the free end with about 12 to 18 hundred pounds, and hinged at the other end to a post firmly dug into the ground. At the bottom of the front part of the press there is an aperture through which the filtered liquid escapes, flowing thence down a gently inclined surface into a receptacle placed below.

The mash (*moromi*) is put into long, hempen bags which have been strengthened by being soaked in *kaki-no-shibu*, the juice of the unripe persimmon.[*]

Each bag is filled about two-thirds full and then contains about 3-1/2 sho; the open end is folded over and tied, and from 300 to 500 bags are piled up in the press according to its size. At Itami there are four presses in use, two of which hold 400 bags, and the other two 342. At Nishinomiya, the press holds 500 bags. At first the weight put upon the lever is very small, otherwise the liquid would run through turbid, but afterwards the weights are increased to 12 or 18 hundred pounds. The pressure is kept up for 12 hours after which the weights are removed, the bags turned over, the pressure renewed for 12 hours longer. The filtrate is slightly turbid and, before use, requires clearing.

At the Tokyo brewery one half of the whole quantity of liquid was filtered on the twenty-seventh, and the remainder before the thirty-second day. A sample of the filtered liquid taken on that day had the following composition:

Alcohol	11.14%
Glycerin, resin, and albumenoids	1.992%
Fixed acid	0.13%
Volatile acid	0.02%
Water (by difference)	86.718%
	100.0%
Specific gravity	0.990

Compared with the mash on the twenty-eighth day it will be observed that the percentage of alcohol is considerably less, a difference caused by the addition to the mash before filtering of the water used by the brewer for the purpose of rinsing out the tuns.

The composition of the pressed residue (*kasu*) was found to be:

Soluble solid matter	1.43%
Starch and cellulose	32.07%
Ash	0.70%
Alcohol	6.0%
Water	59.8%
	100%

The alcohol which is unavoidably left in the residue is extracted at a later period by a process of distillation which will be described on a subsequent page.

The amount of sake obtained by the brewer for the quantities given above for one moto was 6.86 koku of specific gravity 0.99, therefore weighing 326 kuwamme, and the weight of the residue was 58 kw. We are now in possession of all the data required to calculate the efficiency of the brewing process as regards the conversion of the starch used into alcohol.

As the sake contained 11.14% alcohol by weight, the total weight of absolute alcohol contained in 326 kw. was 36.32 kw. The 58 kw. of residue, also, contained 6%, amounting altogether to 3.48 kw.; the total quantity of alcohol, therefore, which the brewer obtained was 39.8 kw.

We have already seen that the materials used for one moto amounted to:

Dry rice	175.1 kw.
Water	329.03 kw
	504.13 kw.

The dry rice contains on average 84% starch, which, if it were completely converted into alcohol would furnish 80 kw. As the amount actually obtained was only 39.8 kw. we see that the yield is not quite one half of that which is theoretically obtainable. In accurate numbers it is 49.75%. That the loss of material during the preparation of the sake is considerable will be evident when the number of transferences from one vessel to another is considered. Two other sources of loss also are very important, the loss of matter by the rice first, during the process of cleaning and washing, and secondly, during the filtration.

The following calculation will furnish us with some guide to the quantity of material lost in these operations. Allowance is made for the carbonic acid evolved by assuming that it amounts to 98% of the alcohol formed. This number is the result of experiments made by many former observers upon the ratio of carbonic acid to alcohol formed during ordinary fermentation. Any difference between it and the truth will be too small to affect the conclusions:*

Total weight of sake obtained	326 kw.
Total weight of residue	58 kw.
Weight of carbonic acid lost	39 kw.
	423 kw

As 504.13 kw. of dry rice and water were used at starting, the total quantity accounted for is only 84%. The weight of dry rice given above was corrected for the loss of weight during the conversion of a part of it into koji, so that the loss of 16% is over and above that experienced during the formation of koji. And indeed, this is not the whole loss because no account is taken of the additional water used in cleaning the vessels, amounting to about 18 kuwamme, which would raise the loss to 19%.

The yield of alcohol obtained at Itami is rather higher than that found in the Tokyo brewery. The quantity of sake obtained is 13.32 koku, which will contain 75.9 kw. of alcohol. 75 kw of residue are also obtained containing 3.8 kw. of alcohol, which altogether amounts to 79.7 kw. The weight of dry rice used we have seen to be 310.77 kw., containing 260.4 kw. of dry starch and ought to produce 140.3 kw. of alcohol. The actual yield is, therefore, 56.8 of that which theory indicates.

At Nishinomiya, the weight of dry rice used is 310.1 kw. and it ought to produce, as at Itami, 140 kw. of alcohol. The yield of sake for one moto is 14.1 koku, which, together with 80 kw. of residue would contain 77.7 kw. of alcohol, and the actual percentage of alcohol obtained is thus 55.5% of that theoretically possible.

There is a very general agreement between the actual yield of alcohol in the three breweries mentioned; although that found by myself as the result of the brewing operation in Tokyo is less than that calculated from the numbers given to me at Itami and Nishinomiya. We may assume that the percentages obtained at Itami and Nishinomiya are the best results, as they ought to be considering the long experience which the brewers of those districts have had. The operations at Tokyo on the other hand are conducted on a much smaller scale and it is scarcely to be expected that the brewers will possess the same skill as those in the great centers of sake production.

Mr. Korschelt, in the paper on sake already referred to*, has mentioned that the actual yield of alcohol according to information from one brewer is only 50% of that theoretically possible, and he expresses the opinion that in any case it is too little, and that the production must reach nearly 100%, because the conversion of starch into sugar is so complete.

I do not consider that the process followed at the Tokyo brewery is a very satisfactory one, but that practised at Itami may be regarded as the one which is carried out with the greatest degree of skill, and yet even there the yield is not more than 57% of that which might be obtained. The case in which Mr. Korschelt says he obtained 80.5% must be exceptional, and I am inclined to think that he has overrated the percentages of alcohol contained in the sake produced. At Itami the strongest sake does not contain, even before dilution, more than 14% alcohol, and it is not probably that the percentage in a Tokyo brew will be greater. In the process which Mr. Korschelt examined in Tokyo, and of which he gives details, the actual yield of sake is 67% of the theoretical yield. The mash consists of the following:

- 2.9 koku of moto
- 3.2 koku of koji
- 12.0 koku of rice
- 13.9 koku of water

This mash contained 475.4 kw. of starch and ought to have yielded 256 kw. of alcohol. The mash just before filtering measured, according to Mr. Korschelt, 25 koku and contained 14.5% alcohol. If we assume that the specific gravity of the mash was 0.99 (as I found in a similar brew), the total weight of the mash would be 1187.5 kw. and would contain 172 kw. of alcohol, that is 67% of the theoretical yield. This yield is certainly greater than the average yield in other breweries, and may have been the result of special precautions on the part of the brewer, but even in this case, only two thirds of the alcohol was obtained.

In an earlier part of his paper Mr. Korschelt has calculated the theoretical composition of the moto, and also of the mash at the end of the principal fermentation, comparing it with the amounts of extract and alcohol actually found. He arrives at the conclusion that the whole of the starch used enters into solution, at any rate, in one of the examples he brings forward. In the case of moto he gives the theoretical percentage of extract as 35.46, while in one batch of moto he finds 36.86%. In none of the other examples does the percentage arrive at such a high point, being as a rule from 26 to 28%.

The method of water contained in freshly made koji, as used by the brewer, varies from 25 to 30% and never falls so low as 15%, which Mr. Korschelt assumes it to contain. The correction for this will cause an increase in the amount of water given in his paper (loc. cit. p. 250) from 2.925 kw. to 6.32 kw. Again, acting on the assumption that the sugar present in the mash is maltose, the weight of water taken up by the starch in conversion to sugar is calculated only as 1/18, whereas, dextrose being present, as I have shown, it should be twice as much, that is instead of being 2.6 kw. it will really be 5.2 kw. This correction acts in the opposite direction in two ways, first by adding to the weight of the extract, and by taking away from the weight of the water.

Further, the assumption is made that the matter other than starch dissolved from the rice will amount only to 2% of the rice, but in reality at least 12% is dissolved. I have found that the presence of the diastatic ferment of koji has the property of rendering the insoluble albumenoids of the rice soluble, and Messrs. Brown and Heron[*] have shown that in the case of malt a certain proportion of the cellulose is held in solution. This will, therefore, add greatly to the concentration of the mash, and finally, the percentage of extract is increased by the removal of water and of carbonic acid during the fermentation. Mr. Korschelt allows 2% for the former, but he omits all correction for the latter. As we have seen however, the weight of carbonic acid evolved is about 98% of the total weight of alcohol formed, in consequence of which the total weight of the mash is diminished by that amount. Hence if the composition of the mash calculated on the supposition that the starch is completely converted into sugar is compared with the actual quantity of extract calculated from solid matter in solution and from alcohol, it is evident that the former will appear too low, and that therefore, the apparent solution of the starch will appear too favorable. This makes a very important item in the calculations, and its non-correction diminishes greatly the accuracy of the results obtained by Mr. Korschelt. The following method of calculating the results avoids the errors which have been pointed out, and shows that the whole of the starch is *not* brought into solution as Mr. Korschelt supposes.

The composition of the mash was given on page page 74, and we saw that it contained 475.4 kw. of pure starch. The weight of the whole brew before filtering was 1187.5 kw. This contained 172 kw. of alcohol, which is equivalent to 1.856 x 172 = 319.6 kw. of dry starch. The mash also contained 6.5% of extract, which we may assume to be entirely dextrin (although this assumption is in favor of the perfection of the method) and would thus weight 0.065 x 1187.5 = 77.2 kw. The sum of the two numbers, 319.6 + 77.2 = 396.8 kw., is the total weight of starch which has been brought into solution. We see, therefore, that only 83.5% of the total starch used has been dissolved.

So far, therefore, from being able to agree with Mr. Korschelt that the "process of sake brewing is so complete, that important improvements cannot be made in it, unless we would alter the ultimate product to such an extent that it would no longer be sake"[*] we ought to conclude from the evidence given in his own paper that it is still capable of being much improved. And this conclusion is born out by all the evidence as to yield which I have been able to obtain, even from the oldest and best managed breweries.

---

[*] For an explanation of the action of this liquid upon cloth and paper, see Ishikawa. Chem. News, Dec. 3, 1880. Transactions of the Asiatic Soc. of Japan, IX, 36.

[*] The escaping carbonic acid must be saturated with water, and will also cause the evaporation of more or less of the alcohol formed, but it is not possible to estimate the amount of this loss with any approach to accuracy, and it is therefore included in the total loss of 16%.

[*] Mittheilungen der deutsches Gessellschaft. 16tes Heft. p. 256.

[*] loc. cit. p. 627.

[*] "Das Verfahren beim Sake Brauen ist an sich so vollkommen, dass bedeutends Verbesserungen darin nicht gemacht werden konnen, wenn man nicht das schliessliche Product so dadurch verandern will, dass so eben nicht mehr Sake ist." (loc. cit., p. 257, English translation from Japan Mail, August 1878).

Chapter 10. Preservation of Sake

CLEARING

The liquid which has passed through the press is turbid and requires clarification before being used. This is effected by collecting the sake in large tuns which have two holes near the bottom one above the other, and closed by means of plugs (see Figure 1). After the lapse of about 15 days the suspended matter has settled to the bottom, and the greater part of the clear liquid may then be drawn off by removing the upper plug, and collecting the liquid in proper vessels. The remainder is allowed to stand for a longer time, and the clear part is separated by opening the lower hole. What remains is termed *ori* and is added to another brew just before filtering.

HEATING

The clear sake so produced would not keep for more than a few days in the warm weather without being subjected to some further process. At Itani and at Nishinomiya the heating of the sake is carried out on the 88th night called *hachiju-hachiya*, which usually occurs between the 24th and 25th of the fourth month of the old calendar. The operation is a very simple one. A large iron pan is built in the ground, so that the upper part is only about 5 or 6 inches above the surface; on one side the ground is cut away, and a fire-place arranged below the pan, the opening being some distance below the floor. The bottom of the pan is heated directly by the flame from a wood fire, and the heating is continued until the liquid is so hot that a workman can just dip in his hand three times in succession without feeling much inconvenience. At some works thermometers have been introduced, and the temperature indicated varies from 120°F to 130°F. Whilst still hot the sake is transferred to the store vats, large tuns holding about 40 koku, made of *sugi* (cryptomeria japonica) or *hinoki* (chamaecyparis obtusa). They are closed by lids and the interval pasted round with paper fastened by means of a kind of glue made from seaweed (*funori*). In these tuns the liquid will keep without alteration so long as the weather remains cold, but as soon as the summer sets in, the sake has to be frequently examined in order to detect any change. When any signs of alteration are apparent it has to be taken out of the tun, and again heated, after which it is returned to the store vat.

In the following table (Table 26) are given analyses of several kinds of sake obtained from the districts of Itami and Nishinomyia. They were in most cases obtained directly from the respective brewers, and may be regarded as pure and unadulterated samples.

The samples of sake of which analyses are given in the table were brewed in the winter of 1879-80, and had been subjected to the operation of heating only once. As will be seen there is not a very great variation in their composition, the percentage of alcohol not passing beyond the limits 11 to 14. The quantities of dextrose and dextrin are very small, and in this circumstance, as well as in the larger percentage of alcohol, lies the essential difference between sake and beer. Connected with the absence of the two latter bodies also is the freedom from carbonic acid, for the sake is quite as still as the most fermented wine. When newly prepared it possesses a pale straw color, and has a peculiar unripe taste, but on keeping, and especially after heating, the color darkens and the taste becomes more matured. During the hot weather it is impossible to prevent the sake "turning" without frequent heating, and as this is a very laborious operation any improvement would be welcomed by the brewer. Several samples which have undergone this change have been examined; it appears to be accompanied by the formation of butyric acid, ammonia, and a volatile, ill-smelling substance, whilst at the same time a portion of the alcohol disappears.

Table 26: Composition of Various Sakes from Itami and Nishinomiya

	Itami				Nishinomiya				
Name of sake	Gaika	Hatsu-hikage	Shira-yuki		Irozakari	Tai-riyo	Saki-gake	Kome-ichi	Zui-ichi
Name of brewer	Konishi Shin-yemon	Konishi Shin-yemon	Konishi Mote		Idzumi Man-suke	Tatsu Gonuske	Tatsu yasu	Tatsuma Kijiro	
Alcohol	12.30	12.15	12.15	13.10	13.73	11.20	12.83	11.00	13.50
Dextrose	0.62	0.312	0.44	0.56	0.404	--	0.82	0.20	1.41
Dextrin	0.255	0.256	0.30	0.05	0.18	0.16	0.22	0.14	0.39
Glycerin, ash,[a] and albumenoids	1.530	2.15	1.857	1.46	1.833	1.81	1.22	1.58	2.02
Fixed acid	0.145	0.13	0.123	0.32	0.143	0.12	0.32	0.13	0.24
Volatile acid	0.015	0.01	0.032	0.03	0.026	--	0.014	0.014	0.013
Water (difference)	85.135	84.992	85.098	84.48	83.684	86.71	84.576	86.936	82.427
	100	100	100	100	100	100	100	100	100
Specific gravity	0.991	0.992	0.992	0.993	0.989	0.990	0.990	0.991	0.994
Rotatory power	36°	25.6°	33°	19.7°	24°	16.4°	37°	20.6°	41.6°
Sign of Saké	凱歌印	初日永印	白雪印	○印	いろ盛印	大漁印	魁印	弘明印	瑞一

a. The ash consists mainly of the phosphates of calcium and magnesium.

One sample which had been allowed to stand from the spring of 1879 until June 1880 contained 11.4% of alcohol and 0.316% of total acid, of which 18% was butyric acid. As the original sake was not completely analyzed I cannot give it for comparison. Two samples of those already given were kept and analyzed after standing in bottles corked in the usual way from February 5th, 1880, until January 17th, 1881, and November 1st, 1880, respectively. The composition of the original sake is repeated alongside for convenience and comparison.

In both cases a diminution in the percentage of alcohol took place after keeping, and at the same time the small quantity of dextrose present in the original sake disappeared. The principal apparent change is the large increase in the percentage of fixed acid, whilst at the same time a small quantity of butyric acid is also formed. It is the presence of this acid together with the volatile body before mentioned which causes the disgusting smell possessed by such "turned" sake, notwithstanding the very small percentage contained in the liquid, but the sour taste of spoilt sake is due to the fixed acid, mainly lactic acid. The quantities of alcohol and dextrose which have disappeared are much greater than the weights of acid formed, a circumstance which shows that a combustion occurs resulting in the formation of carbonic acid and water. In fact the liquid which has been kept over a summer will be found to be highly charged with carbonic acid, whereas unaltered sake contains none.

Table 27: Composition of Itami Sake "Gaika" Before and After Standing

	Before Standing (2/5/1880)	After Standing (1/17/1881)
Alcohol	12.3	11.90
Dextrose	0.62	--
Dextrin	0.255	0.225
Glycerin, ash, etc.	1.53	1.667
Fixed acid	0.145	0.360
Acetic acid	0.015	0.062
Butyric acid	--	0.006
Water	85.135	85.780
	100	100

	Before Standing (2/5/1880)	After Standing (11/1/1880)
Alcohol	13.73	12.48
Dextrose	0.404	--
Dextrin	0.180	1.92
Glycerin, ash, etc.	1.833	
Fixed acid	0.143	0.335
Acetic acid	0.26	0.23
Butyric acid	--	0.53
Water	83.684	85.189
	100	100

At the bottom of the vessel in which the sake has been kept is a thick deposit consisting almost entirely of minute cells some of which are represented in Figure 25 and Figure 26. The organisms in Figure 25 resemble those found in putrid beer, and those in Figure 26 are almost identical with the filaments which produce "turned" beer. The former are more commonly met with, and doubtless, by their growth give rise to the unpleasant odor characteristic of spoilt sake. It is for the purpose of destroying these organisms that the sake is heated, but as, after heating, no precaution is taken to prevent the contact of the liquid with fresh germs, repeated heatings are necessary. Indeed during the hot months from June to September, the sake must be heated at least once a month and very often more frequently.

Figure 25: Ferment cells in spoilt sake from Sakai , x 720.

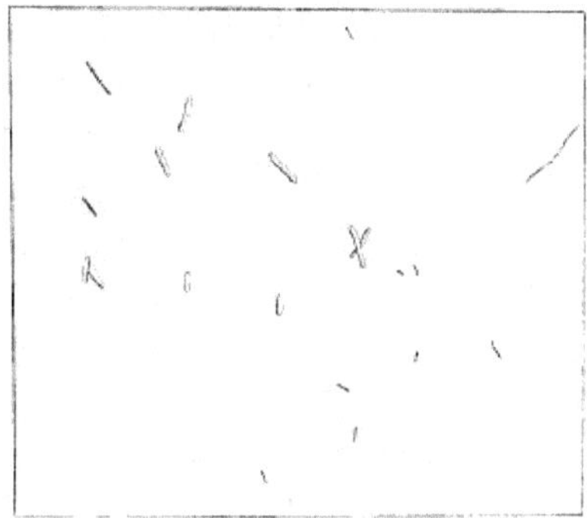

Figure 26: Ferment cells in another specimen of spoilt sake, x720.

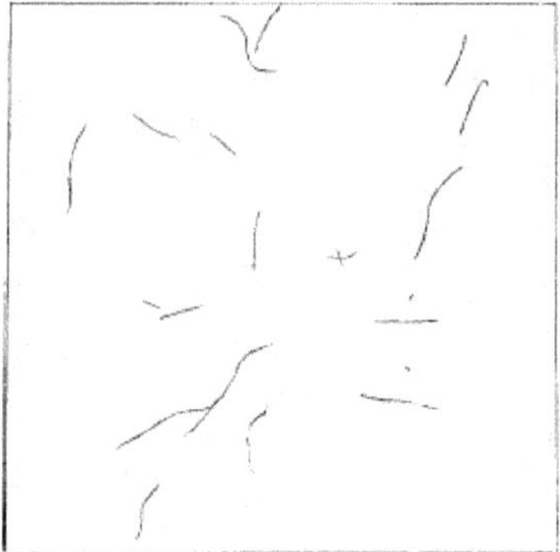

It is an important and interesting fact that the process of heating the sake for the purpose of preserving it has been in use in Japan for about 300 years, and it is all the more remarkable, that having discovered the beneficial effect of this operation, the brewer should not have made it lasting by taking precautions against subsequent contaminations. Instead of doing this, however, the liquid after having been heated is returned to the same store vats in which it was formerly kept, and the sides of which still retain particles of the ferment attached. When the still hot liquid is put into the vat, it is possible that the high temperature will kill all those germs adhering to the sides of the tun so far as the liquid rises. But above the level of the liquid they will remain untouched, and as, during the subsequent standing of the sake, the alcohol is drawn up the sides of the tun and runs back again in the form of "tears", the germs will in that way be carried down into the sake, will slowly develop, and in a comparatively short time will render it undrinkable.

The Japanese brewer has been credited with the discovery of the method of preserving alcoholic liquids which has made the name of M. Pasteur so widely known, but when we consider that in Japan, the heated liquid is allowed to become inoculated with the germs of its disease, even at the time of tis so-called preservation, we see that he has omitted a part of the process which Pasteur truly regards as vital. When an alcoholic liquid has been "pasteurized," as the expression is, it will keep for an indefinite time, because the germs of disease which were already present have been killed by the high temperature of the liquid, and care is subsequently taken that no fresh germs find access to it. A wine thus treated not only does not deteriorate but actually improves by keeping, because it is allowed to "age" without the danger of any malady being set up which would spoil it. The Japanese wine, sake, is not allowed to improve in this way; I have in vain endeavored to get samples which have been preserved for several years. As a rule, even at the most extensive breweries in Itami and Nishinomiya, the whole of the winter's production is consumed within a year, and the reason is evident; it is impossible that the repeated heatings which the sake requires during the summer months in order to prevent it going utterly to decay should be without effect upon its quality. Further the liquid is not heated until the brewer detects an incipient spoiling, which means the already considerable development of ferment with the production of butyric acid, and although a portion of the latter is probably driven away on heating, some is sure to remain. By repeated fermentation and heating, therefore, the amount of butyric constantly increases, and thus in time, the sake must become undrinkable.

A process simple and effective, which will preserve the sake is evidently greatly desired by brewers, as is shown by the many attempts which have been made to use salicylic acid for this purpose. Mr. Korschelt wrote a pamphlet advocating the use of this antiseptic, and succeeded in persuading many large brewers to try it, but so far as I can learn, the success of the experiment has not been such as to satisfy the expectations raised. Salicylic acid has been introduced in Europe of late years as a means of preventing the deterioration of wine and beer, and when employed in sufficient quantity appears to answer the purpose in the climates of England and Germany. Prof. Kolbe mentions that "salicylic acid added to new wine entirely prevented after-fermentation. It appears also to prevent wine kept in half empty bottles becoming stale and sour. The quantity of the acid found sufficient for the purpose was 0.2 gram (or 0.1 gram salicylic acid and 0.1 gram acid potassium sulphate) per bottle." He also gives experiments showing the influence of the presence of differing quantities of salicylic acid upon a light, English beer, which would usually keep for about four months. The quantities added were to 100 liters of the beer.

Table 29: Beer Brewed in January 1875

Weight of salicylic acid added to 100 liters beer[a]	Examined August 1875	Examined December 1875
0	Sour	--
2.5 grams	Not good taste	Sour
5 grams	Good taste and in good condition	Good taste
10 grams	Good, sparkling, and clear; of good taste and aroma	Good in every respect
20 grams	Good, sparkling, clear and full-bodied	Clear, sparkling, and of good aroma. Excellent in every respect
40 grams	Rather too new in taste. Very good.	Like the foregoing, but fuller bodied and very sparkling

a. Abstracts in Journal of the Chem. Society. London, 1876, vol. 1, p. 992. From J. pr. Ch. [2] xiii, 106.

The evidence of the experiments quoted above goes to show that when from 10 to 20 grams of salicylic acid are added to 100 liters of beer, or to about 110,000 grams, i.e., 1 or 2 in 10,000, the preservation is perfect during summers such as we are accustomed in Europe. How far the higher temperature experienced in this country will modify the results we have no means of knowing. The only direct experiments I am acquainted with, besides those of Mr. Korschelt, are mentioned by Prof. Kinch in the Transactions of the Asiatic Society of Japan.[*] He says, "Numerous experiments were made last summer with salicylic acid as an antiseptic agent for sake, and it was found that used in the ratio of 1:10,000 it preserved sake in imperfectly closed vessels for about a month, and when used in the ratio of 1:5000 it preserved the sake through the whole of the summer even under very trying circumstances." This evidence corroborates that offered by Prof. Kolbe, and we must probably look to the quantities used by the brewers for an explanation of their want of success. One of their complaints was the expense of the material, and though I do not know in what proportions it was used, it may readily be imagined that they would err on the side of deficiency rather than on the opposite side.

Although the evidence in favor of the action of salicylic acid in arresting the change of alcoholic liquids, experiments have been conducted only for a comparatively short time, and there is nothing to show that the effect is a permanent one. Indeed from the chemical properties of salicylic acid, and especially from the readiness with which it is converted into salicylic ether in presence of alcohol and an acid, it may be regarded as certain that when a solution of the acid in sake is allowed to remain for a considerable time, especially at the summer temperature, it will be transformed into salicylic ether, and as this body probably does not possess the same antiseptic properties as the acid, the preservative effect of the acid will thus prove to be only temporary. Moreover the wood of the vessel in which such liquids are kept has been shown gradually to absorb the acid and thus destroy its utility. These circumstances will however, only necessitate the more frequent addition of salicylic acid, and as Prof. Kinch has shown that 1 part in 5000 of sake is sufficient to prevent the liquid spoiling during a whole summer it is only necessary that this amount should be added each spring the make the process successful. So long, however, as the price of salicylic acid is as high as it is at present in Japan, it will probably be more economical to heat the sake with such modifications in the form of the apparatus as will presently be described.

It is not necessary to wait until salicylic acid falls in price sufficiently to make its use economical; the brewer has at hand all the appliances needful for making his brew keep as long as he pleases, and without any additional expense further than that required to alter the shape of some of his vessels. I have pointed out that the weak point of the present method is that the liquid after having been heated is poured back into the same vessel in which it had formerly become spoilt, and that the vessel is *not completely filled*. With the present form of vat used for storing sake it would be difficult, if not impossible, to completely fill it, and be sure that it was also perfectly tight, but if, instead of using the large, upright tuns which are covered by large, flat plates, 6 or 8 feet in diameter, and closed round the edges by means of paper and glue, a vessel were used with only a small bung hole at the upper side which would permit of being easily and securely fastened, the brewer need hardly wish for any other means of preserving sake. At present even at the largest brewery in Itami not much more than 1000 koku (180,000 liters) of sake are prepared in one season, but if proper means of preservation were employed, that amount might be largely increased, say to one million liters or 5500 koku. If the sake were distributed into small barrels holding, say 1 koku each, the number required in one brewery would not be greater than the space would admit of, with this advantage, that even if one barrel went bad the rest of the brew would not be affected. That the heating and preservation of the sake under the conditions mentioned above suffice to prevent the liquid spoiling has been shown by direct experiments with two sorts of sake, one from Itami, "Gaika", and the other from Nishinomyia, "Irozakari." Five bottles of each were heated in a vessel of water until the temperature of the contents rose to 60°C and were then tightly corked and sealed. At the end of twelve months the sake remained clear and brilliant, and had in no way deteriorated, whilst the same sake kept in a bottle closed in the ordinary way was completely spoilt, the change being indicated by the analyses in Table 27 and Table 28. This is evidence, although quite unnecessary, that the process applied to wines is likewise capable of application to sake.

An arrangement for heating sake which would be neither expensive to erect nor liable to get out of order is represented in Figure 27, kindly furnished by Prof. Ewing. It consists of a long, wrought iron box (A), about six feet long, three feet deep, and three feet broad, made of boiler plate riveted together, and built over a small fireplace with flues circulating beneath and on both sides so that the whole of the vessel is pretty equally heated by the hot gases before they escape to the chimney. The right hand side shows a section taken through the furnace some distance beyond the fireplace; the flue beneath is made broader than it would be at the fireplace and to prevent the front part of the wrought iron vessel burning away too rapidly it would be necessary to protect it from immediate contact with the flame by brickwork, which, however, is not represented in the drawing, and need only extend a short distance from the fireplace. In order to support the heating vessel it would be advisable to build up brick pillars in the middle of the flue, but it would not be necessary to make them very broad. The vessel is provided with a lid which can be removed when it is required to clean the inside; it has in the center a long opening, somewhat larger at one end, which is usually covered with wooden plates. The larger square opening (b) is for the introduction of the sake to be heated; the longer one for the purpose of stirring the liquid in order to equalize the temperature as much as possible. That there may be no danger of the iron becoming burnt by the exposure of its sides to the action of the hot air when there is no liquid within to protect it, it will always be found advisable to withdraw the fire from the grade before removing the heated sake. A vessel of the size given will hold about 8 koku of hot sake. To permit the withdrawal of the sake and its introduction into proper vessels which may be completely filled with it while still hot, a pipe is led through the brickwork and reaches some distance beyond it ending in a stopcock and curved neck, the vertical portion being made to slide up and down so that it may allow of the passage under it of a barrel in the way shown in the diagram. At the side of the furnace a depression in the ground is made in such a way that the barrel, resting upon a small barrow, can be wheeled down an inclined plane on one side and be brought right under the tap, and when filled can be pushed forward, and its place taken by a fresh one, and so on until the greater part of the liquid has been stored. As soon as the barrel is filled it is, of course, tightly closed in the usual way. The barrels which would be suitable for this purpose are such as are used in beer breweries, and some very good examples are shown by the Kai tak shi (Colonization Department) in the present National Exhibition (1881).

In Figure 28, a form of apparatus for heating wine, devised by M. Rossignol[*] is shown, taken, by kind permission of the author, from M. Pasteur's work on wine, p. 232 (Ed. of 1873). The following is a translation of the description which accompanies the drawing. "This apparatus consists of three parts: 1.) a furnace F, which does not differ from any ordinary furnace; 2.) a broad, copper boiler C. provided with a cover soldered to it, and prolonged into a straight tube H, open at the end: the apparatus is filled with water half up the tube, and serves as a water bath; 3.) a wooden trough or barrel T, the bottom of which is awn off, and which rests upon the edge of the lid of the boiler and is firmly fastened to the cover by a simple arrangement: the edge of the cover a extends beyond the boiler for 3 or 4 centimeters; below it is a ring of wrought iron, and above a washer of caoutchouc, upon which rests the edge of the barrel; an iron ring encircles the edge of the barrel and is provided with straps of iron e which are fastened to the lower ring by strong bolts. The interval between the outside of the boiler and the inside of the barrel is filled with the wine, and all that portion of the boiler with which the wine comes in contact is tinned. A thermometer t indicates the temperature of the wine; a vessel E with tube allows the apparatus to be completely filled and the wine to expand on heating. A simple glance at the figure will explain how the apparatus works. It heats 6 hectoliters (3.3 koku) in 1 hour, uses 10 centimes (10 sen) of fuel per hectoliter, and costs 140 francs."

Figure 27: Apparatus for heating sake.

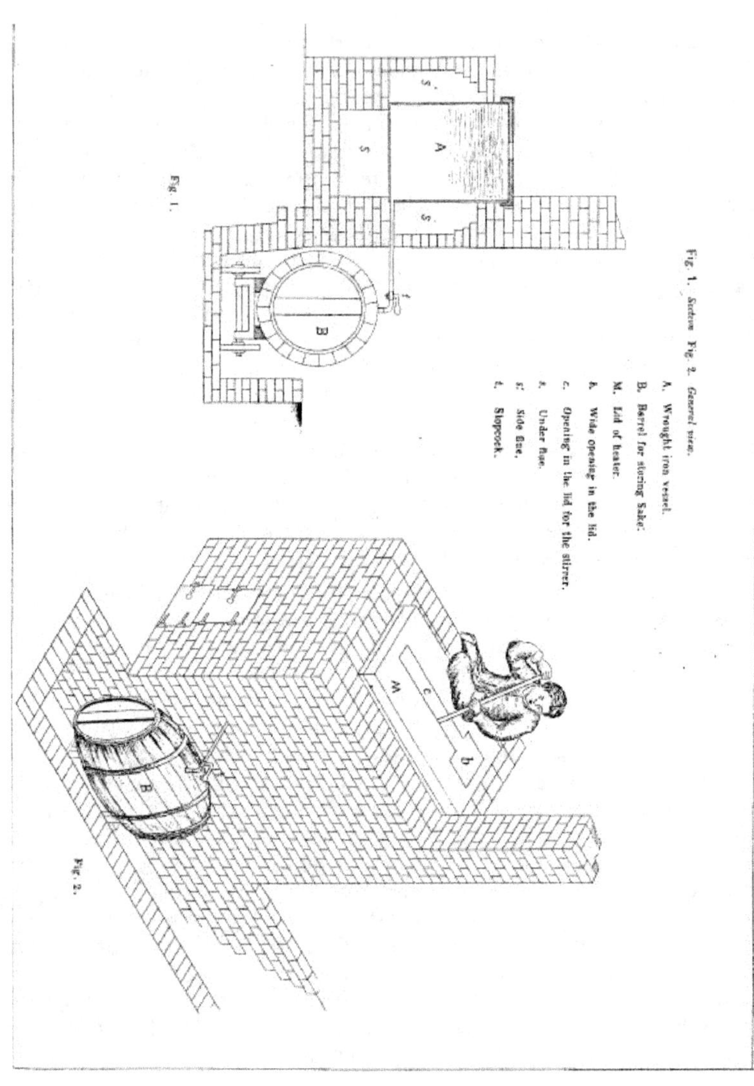

Figure 28: Rossiquel's apparatus for heating wine.

This apparatus like the one before mentioned, has the disadvantage of being intermittent. The following description applies to the apparatus of M. Terrel des Chenes, shown in Figure 29, also taken from M. Pasteur's "Etudes sur le vin", p. 245. Figure 30 shows the arrangement of casks and heating apparatus at work. The heat generator consists of:

1. A central fire box F in the form of a truncated cone; the fire occupies the lower part. The fuel is introduced at first through the side opening P, and when the apparatus is at work, through the small door P' made in the chimney. A register moderates the draft.

2. A water batch B, which occupies the whole of the interval between the fire box and the outer cylinder. v is a clearing cock. Above the bath is a reservoir open to the air, constantly full of water, separated from the water bath by means of a horizontal partition, and communicating with it by a valve o attached to a lever. The lever itself is connected with the stopcock v by means of a chain; when from any accidental cause the temperature of the bath rises too high, the vapor escapes through o, the water enters and the bath is

brought back to the normal temperature and is fed at the same time. If, for any reason, the apparatus has to be stopped for any time and the temperature of the bath rises too much, the same result is attained by opening the stopcock v which raises the valve o, the cold water which is always kept in the open reservoir enters the bath and cools it.

3. A worm ss, through which the wine flows; this consists of 40 small copper tubes, 4 millimeters in internal diameter, which open at one end at the mouth N, at the other at K, after having made nearly two turns in the water batch. The cooler RR is formed of a very large pipe surrounding the heat generator, containing inside 40 small parallel tubes s', 4 millimeters in diameter, like those within the bath. They open at one end into a box H, in which a thermometer dips to indicate the temperature, and at the opposite end of the wide tube into a cavity, R.

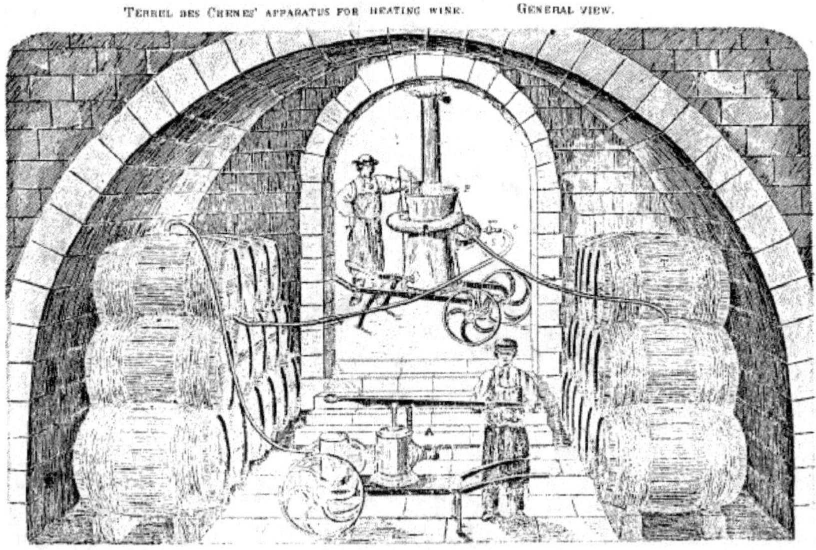

Figure 30: Terrel des Chenes' apparatus for heating wine—general view.

When in action the wine flows in the following way through the apparatus. The cold wine enters by the tube a into R in the wide gland which forms the cooler, circulates on the outside of the small tubes in RR; and leaves at N' by a tube passing at once into the heat generator; traverses the 40 tubes ss of the apparatus, leaves it at K and enters the cooler by the tube l, flows through the 40 small tubes s's' (cooled by the newly arrived cold wine) and finally leaves the heating apparatus by the tube e. Figure 30 presents a perspective view of the complete apparatus and the mode of using it. It is represented by B at the opening of the cellar; it is borne upon a barrow and may be moved by one man; an air pump A, also supported upon a barrow, is used to compress the air in the upper part of the cask T, the wine contained in which is to be heated; a pipe inserted in the lower part of the cask brings the wine to e in the heating apparatus B; another pipe S conducts the heated wine into an empty cask T'.

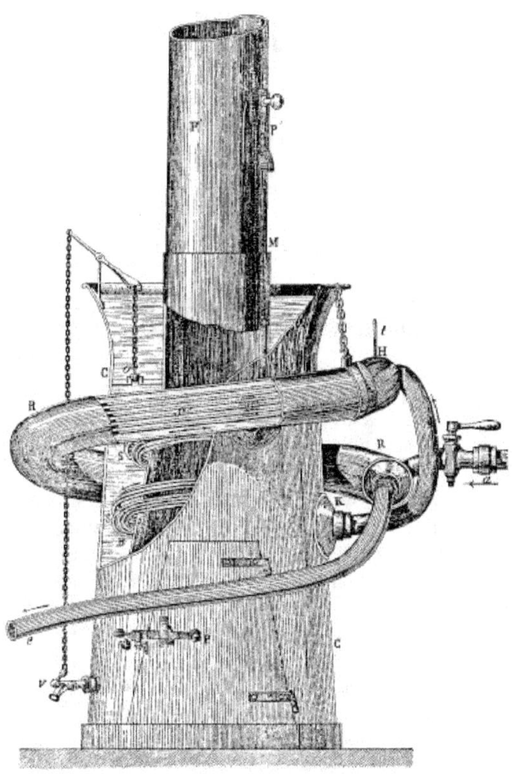

Figure 29: Terrel des Chenes apparatus for heating wine.

To set the whole at work the water bath is filled, the wine is forced into the apparatus by working the pump; and when the water is hot enough, the stopcock S is slightly opened: the thermometer rises; when it reaches 60°, for example, the stopcock is opened more, and then only is the wine received into the empty cask. One man works the pump, while another takes charge of the heating apparatus and regulates the flow of the wine by means of the stopcock, watching the thermometer all the time.

When, the operation ended, the apparatus has to be cleaned, the valve o is unscrewed, and in its place the extremity of the tube e is inserted; a current of stream then passes through the apparatus in a direction opposite to the flow of the wine, and drags away the deposit which has formed in the tubes.

The following data will given an idea of the economical results of this apparatus:

	Price, with all requisites	Number of hectoliters heated per hour to 60°
Large apparatus	1200 francs	10
Medium size	450 francs	5
Small	220 francs	less than 1

The large apparatus receiving the wine at 15°C raises it to 60° and cools it to 32°C. It requires 5 kilos of coal per hour, costing 1-1/2 centime per hectoliter; its diameter at the base is 0.50 meter, its total height 2 meters. The total weight with pump and other requisites does not exceed 230 kilos.

At present as the sake cannot be preserved without alteration for any length of time, the beneficial results of "ageing" have not been experienced, and a decided improvement in the quality of the liquid may be looked forward to by the adoption of the heating and preserving in well closed, wooden barrels. One effect would be that a quantity of air would diffuse through the wood and would mature the wine without the danger of any disease germs accompanying it. The influence of oxygen upon wine cannot be better described than in Pasteur's own words.* "In my opinion it is oxygen which makes the wine; it is by its influence that the wine ages; it modifies the bitter constituents of new wine, and causes the bad taste to disappear; it is the same agent which induces the formation of deposits of good character in casks and in bottles, and far, indeed, from an absorption of a few cubic centimeters of oxygen per liter of wine spoiling it, removing from it its "bouquet" and weakening it, I believe that wine has not come to its proper state, and should not be bottled, so long as it has not absorbed an amount of oxygen much greater than that."

---

* Vol. VIII, p.407.

* I know, the figure says "Rossiquel". I think the original mss. has a typo. *MAS*

* Etudes sur le vin. 1873, p. 85.

Chapter 11. Shochu and Mirin

In a former section it was mentioned that the residue of undissolved starch and cellulose, left behind after pressing the mash, contained about 6% alcohol, and that the brewer made use of a method which enabled him to recover the greater part of it. This is effected by a process of distillation whereby a kind of spirit called shochu is obtained, which contains, according to certain variations in the treatment, from 20 to more than 40% absolute alcohol. The apparatus used is represented by the accompanying woodcut (Figure 31) and is in principle the same as the small earthenware still, here called *rambiki*, much used in pharmacy. It consists of a shallow, iron basin built over a common fireplace in which wood is burnt, and provided with a flange upon which a wooden cylinder with a perforated bottom rests. Upon the top of this cylinder or tub there is fitted an iron basin terminating below in a point immediately above a kind of flat funnel, the tube of which bends away at an angle, and leads outside the tub to a receiver. The iron basin, when filled with cold water, serves as a condenser and the alcohol which collects upon the under surface, runs down to the point and from that drips into the funnel and then flows outside into the receiver. The condenser A is 24 inches in diameter in the still used at Itami, the wooden tub T, 21-1/2 inches in diameter and 26 inches in height. In other places the dimensions vary a little, thus at Hachioji the condenser is 21 inches in diameter, and 15 inches at the deepest part, the tub is 34 inches high, and in diameter a little less than the condenser. About five of these stills are placed side by side, and the water required for cooling is obtained from a bamboo pipe S leading from a cistern, and having a hole closed by a plug for each condenser. 10 kuwamme of the residue (*kasu*) are mixed with 1.1 kw. of the husk of rice; the quantities used are, however, not usually weighed, but are measured in a wooden tub 20 inches in diameter and 13 inches high, two of which hold 10 kuwamme. The mixture is then placed in the tub upon a hempen cloth which covers the perforated bottom; the boiler is filled with water and the tub is then placed in position, the junction being made tight by means of a straw ring. The condenser is then placed upon the top of the tub, and is filled with water by withdrawing the plug from the bamboo pipe S. The fire is lighted, and as soon as the water boils the vapor rises through the mixture of residue and husk, the latter being used for the purpose of keeping the whole porous. The heat is so regulated that when the water boils, that in the condenser never does more than simmer, and the condensed water and alcohol drop onto the funnel and are collected outside. The water in the condenser is changed several times during an operation lasting one hour, and according to the number of times the water is changed does the strength of the distilled liquid vary; this gives the name to the spirit produced which may be san jo dori (collected in three sho), go jo dor, or shichi-jo-dori (collected in five and seven sho, respectively). For the preparation of the first named spirit, the water is removed 2-1/2 times, for the second 3 times, and 4-1/2 times for the third; for the production of the latter the fire is not urged so much, so that the operation is somewhat prolonged, and of course, more water condenses.

Figure 31: Distilling apparatus.

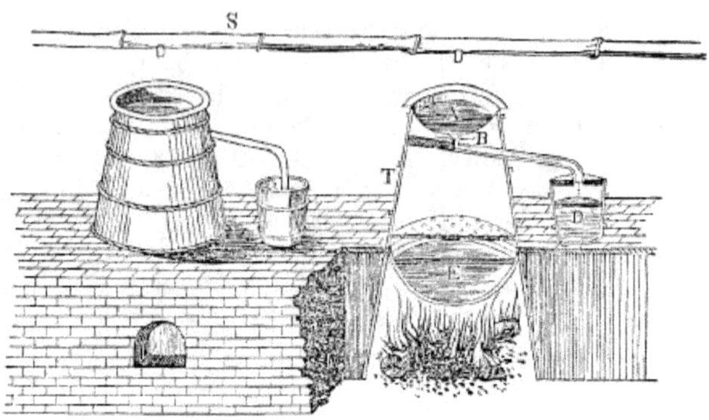

When any of the sake which has been brewed becomes spoilt, the alcohol which it contains is recovered by putting it into the boiler instead of water, and the process of distillation is then conducted in the way above described.

The following are the percentages of alcohol and the specific gravities of some specimens from various places; the liquids contained mere traces of soluble solid matter.

Table 30: Analyses of Spirit (Shochu)

	Kansei from Iyo	Awomori	Hachiobori	Itami 3-sho-dori	Itami 5-sho-dori
Alcohol percentage	50.2	36.99	43.37	41.5	26.00
Specific gravity	0.918	0.942	0.937	0.941	0.964

The residue left after distilling off the alcohol is sold for use as a manure.

The principal use to which this spirit is put is in the preparation of *mirin*, a kind of liquer, which is much drunk at the New Year, and is also largely used for cooking purposes.

The following table gives the composition of a good many different kinds of mirin from different parts, each having a distinctive character: the majority retain merely the aroma received in the ordinary process of manufacture, others, however, are flavored with special materials such as plum juice, and the laves of certain scented herbs.

Most of the above specimens were yellow, thick, somewhat oily liquids, having a sweet, alcoholic taste, and with a peculiar aroma. The two last were specially flavored, the m'meshu possessed a pleasant, acid taste, and a smell of plums, both given to it by digesting the liquer with sour plums. The shisso-shu had a flavor somewhat resembling that of cinnamon, given to it by digestion with the leaves of the Perilla arguta, called in Japanese *shisso*.

Table 31: Composition of Various Kinds of Mirin (Liquer)

	Seven year mirin	Homei-shu	Kuwa-zake Iyo	Yoroshu Iyo	Kanro-shu	Nagare-yama	M'me-shu	Shisso-shu
Alcohol	11.4	12.25	12.50	12.85	13.20	10.00	13.15	18.50
Dextrose	19.32	21.91	17.80	22.50	19.32	30.10	17.92	19.45
Dextrin, etc.	4.04	5.67	2.32	3.06	10.54	4.96	1.94	0.79
Volatile acid	-	-	-	-	-	-	0.005	-
Fixed acid	-	-	-	-	-	-	0.14	0.004
Water	65.24	60.17	67.38	61.59	56.94	54.94	66.845	61.256
	100	100	100	100	100	100	100	100
Specific gravity	1.0801	1.0876	1.0651	1.0877	1.1076	1.1380	1.0613	0.1563
Japanese name and symbol	七年味淋	保命酒	桑酒	養老酒	甘露酒	流山味淋	梅酒	紫草酒

The mode of preparation of mirin depends upon the principles laid down in the first part of this document as to the influence of koji upon starch, but the process differs from that followed in the making of sake, inasmuch as, owing to the presence of the large quantity of alcohol contained in shochu fermentation does not set in, and the chemical changes, therefore, are limited to the solvent action upon starch.

At Itami the following mixture is made:

Steamed *mochigome* (glutinous rice)	9.0 koku
Koji	3.3 koku
Shochu (5 sho dori)	14.0 koku
	26.3 koku

The mixture is put into a large tub and stirred every two days for a period of twenty days, after which a fresh quantity of shochu, amounting to 0.70 koku, is added; the whole is allowed to stand for two days more, stirred, allowed to settle, the clear liquid decanted, and the residue passed through filtering bags. The total quantity of mirin obtained is 21 koku, and the residue amounts to 180 kuwamme, so that, assuming the specific gravity of the mirin to be 1.07, the total weight of mirin and residue will be 1258.5 kuwamme. The total weight of mochigome, koji, and shochu used, including the water taken up during steaming amounts to 1313 kuwamme, thus there is a deficiency of 54.5 kuwamme. This may in part be accounted for by the necessity of using average numbers in the calculation as for the weight of rice, the specific gravity of mirin, etc. At Ozaka the process is quite similar, but the proportions of the materials used differ somewhat; the following are the amounts:

Steamed mochigome (glutinous rice)	7.00 koku
Koji	2.50 koku
Shochu	18.40 koku
	27.90 koku

This quantity is allowed to stand for 15 or 20 days and is stirred every three days. 24 koku of mirin are obtained and 120 kuwamme of residue, altogether weighing 1352 kuwamme while the materials used weight, according to calculations, 1340 kuwamme, a sufficiently close agreement considering the necessity of guessing more or less at the numbers. If we calculate the percentage of alcohol which should be contained in the mirin on the assumption that the shochu used contained 25% by weight of alcohol, and that 6 percent remained in the residue, the percentage in the Itami mirin ought to be 16%, and in that made at Ozaka, 16.6%. As the average percentage is much less than this it shows that the strength of the shochu used must be less than that found for go-sho-dori, and secondly, that there can be no fermentation in the process, as indeed could be seen from the strength of the spirit used. The change which does occur is the conversion of the starch of the rice into dextrose and dextrin; if the whole of the starch contained in the rice used at Ozaka were converted into dextrose, it would form 300 kuwamme which would yield a liquid containing 24.3% dextrose, a number which is not far from those actually found in many specimens.